Internet Information Server (IIS) 6.0 Fundamentals

A Guide to Understanding and Implementing
IIS 6.0 on Windows Server 2003

Michael J. Ware

CG Press Ltd.

ISBN 1-59109-900-5

This publication attempts to provide accurate and authoritative information in regard to the subject matter covered. It is sold with the understanding that the publisher is not engaged in professional services. If professional advice or other expert assistance is required, the services of a competent professional person should be sought.

The author may have patents or pending patent applications, trademarks, copyrights, or other intellectual property rights that relate to the presented subject matter. The furnishing of documents and other materials and information does not provide any license, express or implied, by estoppel or otherwise, to any such patents, trademarks, copyrights, or other intellectual property rights.

The author may make changes to specifications, product descriptions, and plans at any time, without notice.

The author and publisher specifically disclaim any responsibility for any liability, loss, or risk, personal or otherwise, which is incurred as a consequence, directly, or indirectly, of the use and application of any of the contents of this book.

Fictitious names of companies, products, people, characters, and/or data mentioned herein are not intended to represent any real individual, company, product, or event.

Windows Server 3.0, 3.5, 3.51, 4.0, 2000, 2003, .Net, Internet Information Server, SharePoint, and SQL Server are trademarks or registered trademark of Microsoft Corporation

Intel, Itanium, XEON and Pentium are trademarks or registered trademark of Intel Corporation.

† Other names and brands may be claimed as the property of others.

Publisher: CG Press Ltd.
Editor: Dinaz Engineer
Associate Editor: James Ware
Graphic Art: Hackz Publishing

Updates and corrections may be found at: www.hackz.com/IIS6FUN/

Library of Congress Cataloging in Publication Data:
Pending
Printed in the United States of America

10 9 8 7 6 5 4 3 2 1

To my parents, who instilled the discipline in me that made this book possible.

Acknowledgements

Books about new software products are often a challenge to write, this one was no exception. These types of books are usually written using beta software. This software often does not function as expected, leaving the author to wonder if some of the functionality will be changed or removed in the next release. Inevitably, there are major changes between the release candidates and the final released product. These issues require a technical writer to rely on reviewers and technical validators more than would normally be required for a typical technical book.

I have numerous people to thank for their contributions to this book. I would be remiss if I didn't first mention my wife, Michelle. For over a year she sacrificed the majority of what should have been our quality time. She provided emotional support during problems and the eventual change of my original publisher. Most of all, she accepted my need to complete this book.

Officially, this book had no technical or content manager. In reality, Honesto Vargas filled both of these roles. Without the countless hours he spent consulting and proofreading, this book would have never seen the light of day.

I would also like to thank everyone else who contributed to this book by providing copy-editing, technical validation, advice or support. Listed in no particular order: Chris Stanfield, Curtis Hahn, Harold Tamburro, Rob Wallace, Nora Valencia, Charles Eden, Carl Mailman, David Spencer, Mathew Wagner, and everyone else whom I have undoubtedly forgotten to acknowledge.

Table of Contents

Chapter 1

Why Internet Information Server 6.0?

This book demonstrates the advances offered by Microsoft's latest version of Internet Information Server (IIS). A thorough reading will reveal how to get up and running with IIS 6.0, Network Load Balancing Services (NLBS), as well as Microsoft's Application Center on Windows Server 2003. Additionally, Microsoft's implementation of FTP SMTP, and NNTP functionality will be explained.

This book offers the level of detail that an experienced administrator desires, while addressing the reader in a simple and straightforward manner that even inexperienced users will comprehend. It will cover the underlying technology that drives IIS 6.0, as well as the benefits that can be obtained from its proper utilization. Detailed installation and configuration steps are thoroughly documented and illustrated. Finally, advanced techniques and practices are explained with architectural examples that will assist in determining the proper deployment configuration parameters.

Creating a Virtual Enterprise

Companies are looking for more than just a stable web server. They want load balancing, failover, content management, and simplified application integration just as a basic requirement. A Virtual Enterprise can be more than just a collection of web servers; it can be an entire application solution comprising backend, management and transaction processing tiers. A Virtual Enterprise is a complete hosting solution that enables IT organizations to take their enterprise architecture to the next level, combining the best attributes of IIS 6.0 and Windows Server 2003.

In a Virtual Enterprise servers, virtual hosts, Internet sites, intranet gateways—even workstations and Personal Data Assistances (PDAs)—are combined to form a seamless solution. This creates a simple and hassle-free experience for the end user. In a Virtual Enterprise, multiple servers share the burden of providing services. Therefore, a single server failure will not result in a complete application outage. Since a server can be taken offline without affecting application availability, upgrade projects and routine maintenance no longer require downtime. Thanks to this integration, change control processes and maintenance windows are greatly reduced. This reduction in downtime results in increased productivity, while making the delivery of five nines (99.999% uptime) within reach.

While no two Virtual Enterprises are configured exactly the same, one of the main ideas behind a Virtual Enterprise is the notion of destroying the one- server, one-application, one-I.P. address concept. This concept is the idea that each server in the data center has one public IP address and only runs one application. With the notable exception of web servers, this model is practically the universal standard deployment in all enterprise-class networks. Generally, only small companies with isolated networks attempt using a single server for double duty, such as a single server running both file and web services.

Virtual Websites

Before the implementation of the HyperText Transfer Protocol (HTTP)/1.1[1] all web servers required one I.P. address for each second-level domain (e.g., http://foo.com). Therefore, a server with a single network connection that was running ten websites required ten IP addresses, one for each web domain. The implementation of HTTP/1.1 allows web servers, like Microsoft's Internet Information Server (IIS) and Unix's Apache, to share one IP address with many different web domains (Figure 1.1). This sharing of IP addresses is accomplished by adding an identifying line known as a *host header entry* to the web server. The host header entry helps the server

---

1. RFC 2616, http://www.w3.org/Protocols/HTTP/1.1/rfc2616.pdf

identify which of the websites on a shared IP address the user is attempting to access. Even though HTTP/1.1 makes the practice of using separate IP addresses for each different web domain obsolete, a large number of web service providers still operate by providing one IP address per web domain.

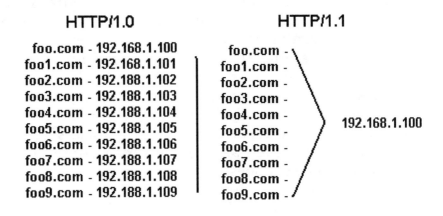

Figure 1.1: Virtual Domains with HTTP /1.1

In a Virtual Enterprise websites can be setup to run on a virtual IP address. Two servers can host, for example, three different websites. However, each server only has a single IP address connected to the Internet. Both servers also share one virtual IP address, an IP address that is valid on the Internet, but is not owned solely by any one server. In this example (Figure 1.2) Microsoft's Network Load Balancing Service (NLBS) manages this virtual IP address. NLBS provides simple load balancing functions and automatic failover in case of a system failure. When users attempt to connect to a website such as foo.com, the DNS entry actually points them to the virtual IP address. NLBS keeps track of which server the user's original request is directed to, enabling that server to keep track of session information, such as cookies and logon credentials. Microsoft's Application Center extends this functionality to content management and dynamic load balancing. These features enable a virtual web farm to easily manage scalability, administration, and availability issues.

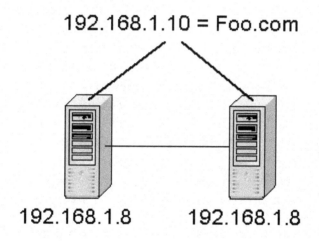

Figure 1.2: NLBS enables Load Balancing

XML is the Key to Making it All Work Together

XML has been a buzzword in the computing industry for the last several years. Only now is it starting to deliver on its promise of easing interoperability while controlling costs. XML is key to enable the different parts of a Virtual Enterprise to work together as one well-oiled machine. Microsoft has built support for XML standards in the foundation of IIS 6.0. XML gives systems a simple and standardized communications medium regardless of their platform or programming language.

XML Web Services

XML works with SOAP (Simple Object Access Protocol) and UDDI (Universal Description, Discovery, and Integration) to provide XML Web Services. XML Web Services are a set of standardized protocols that enable different client applications to communicate using a universal communications medium. This universal communications medium significantly simplifies integration. SOAP is a lightweight protocol based on XML standards that enables applications or services to make and process requests made from other applications and services. UDDI is a service that acts like a huge directory allowing systems all over the Internet to discover and then communicate with each other. XML Web Services automatically register with UDDI to enable easy access for all users.

XML and SOAP were designed to be simple to implement and manage, yet powerful enough to provide a viable solution to real-world interoperability problems. XML Web Services work with the standard protocols used in today's enterprise networks—XML (of course), HTTP, and TCP/IP. Because of the simplicity of XML web services, programming XML-based solutions is very cost-effective and usually does not require a major development project.

Using the example of an online DVD store, the benefits of using XML web services to create a Virtual enterprise can be demonstrated. In this example Dan sells DVDs over the Internet on his website, DansDiscountDVD.com.

Naturally, Dan has a website setup where he sells his DVDs. To track his stock, Dan has an inventory database. Dan also has a system in place to order more DVDs from his supplier when he runs out of stock. Dan has another database for customer records, order history, e-mail addresses, and such. He has an accounting system, to keep track of how much money he is making. Lastly, Dan has a system set up with the shipping company that ships his orders. Keeping all these systems updated could easily be a full-time job for Dan. He needs to update his website whenever he sells out a DVD title. He also often needs to re-order more copies of DVDs from his supplier. Dan then needs to enter the cost and profit from his sales into his accounting database.

If Dan forgets one of these steps, or makes a simple error, it will eventually cause a problem. Let's say Dan forgets to update his inventory database when he makes a sale. Later that day, a customer purchases the same DVD title that Dan forgot to update. Dan's website shows the title as being in stock, his inventory database tells him he has one left, but no matter where Dan looks he cannot find it. The reality is that manual proc-

XML Web Services Overview

- **Universal Data Format**

- **Cuts Development Costs**

- **Simplified Integration**

esses like these not only cost Dan time, they also introduce opportunities for error.

After much frustration, Dan decides to connect his company's systems via XML Web Services, creating his own Virtual Enterprise. When he connects this Website to his inventory database Dan's website can be automatically updated when he runs out of stock. Additionally, by connecting his inventory database to his supplier Dan can automatically order additional stock as needed. If Dan also connects his accounting and shipping systems via XML Web Services, he can automatically track orders, costs, and subtract returns from his profit. XML was designed to address the issues businesses encounter when enabling disparate systems to exchange useful information.

Downsizing the Enterprise

Another way to enable a Virtual Enterprise is by downsizing your network. This can be accomplished by combining multiple websites on a single server, creating application clusters, or by having one server do the work originally done by multiple database servers. IIS 6.0's stability and Windows Server 2003 makes them an ideal choice when downsizing a network.

A common example of migrating from a three-tier architecture to a two-tier architecture is shown in Figure 1.3. This configuration is for a data pipe consisting of database, *Extraction Transform and Load* (ET&L), and presentation tiers. In this example a total of eight servers are used for the backend database and ET&L functions. Combining the backend and ET&L tiers into a single tier on the Xeon, or Itanium processor platform, results in a net reduction of four servers (Figure 1.4). The reduction in decreased manpower for server administration alone can save tens of thousands of dollars a year.

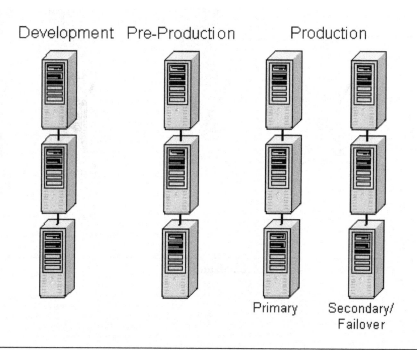

Figure 1.3: Three-tier architecture

Substantial cost savings can be obtained by leveraging high-powered servers to enable this move from a three-tier architecture to a two-tier architecture. With this high cost-effectiveness possible, the importance of closely examining one's current enterprise environment for consolidation opportunities quickly becomes evident.

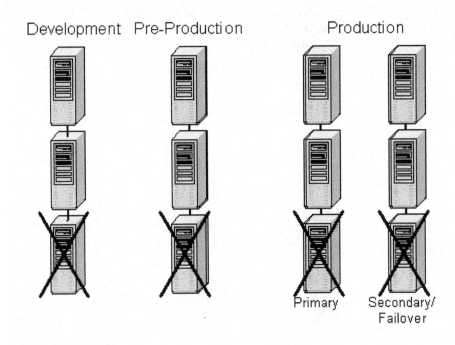

Figure 1.4: Two Tier Architecture

Summary

IIS 6.0 is an ideal platform for web hosting. By leveraging Windows Server 2003 components such as FTP, SQL, and SharePoint, a virtual enterprise that offers a complete application solution can be created. If properly implemented, Microsoft's IIS 6.0 provides a stable, secure and flexible solution for the enterprise.

At least one thing all virtual enterprises have in common is that they look at network architecture in a new way: not as a collection of servers and switches, but as a single integrated system designed from the ground up to deliver reliable, cost-effective services to the end user. This book assists IT professionals in determining how to best implement the latest technology to create a Virtual Enterprise and leverage IIS 6.0.

Chapter 2

Internet Information Server 6.0 Features

Users expect fresh, up-to-date information, they want to see new content on a website literally every time they visit. This places a constant burden on developers to continually update website code, leaving little time for bug tracking and validation testing. As a result, most administrators see a substantial number of failures caused bby bad ASP (Active Server page) code. Therein lies the problem; system administrators are responsible for keeping the website running 24 hours a day, 7 days a week, yet they have little—if any—control over the stability (or lack of it) of the developer's code. IIS 6.0 addresses this issue by totally re-designing the way IIS handles application code.

IIS 6.0 Overview

With today's constantly changing websites, code can never be 100% bug-free. Unfortunately, under IIS 5.0 an error on one website could bring down every site hosted on that server, each website giving out a 503 (Service unavailable) error to clients. The quick fix for this was to place troublesome code in high isolation. Placing code in high isolation runs the code as a separate thread under an isolated process. If code on a website running in high isolation mode fails, it will not interrupt the service of other websites on the server. The problem with running code in high isolation is that it places an increased demand on the CPU and can cause a substantial performance decrease for the entire server. Also, developers may know that if their code causes an issue on the web server they can always have the code run in high isolation. Using isolation mode as a crutch may help developers meet deadlines, but greatly reduces server stability. This makes the developer look good for meeting deadlines, but the system engineers and administrators look bad because of server instability.

This single issue of server stability has kept IIS 5.0 from being utilized as a shared application in most enterprise networks. A shared website under IIS means that bad code on one website can crash every website hosted on the server. In a Virtual Enterprise shared application space is the

IIS 6.0 Features

- **Isolation**

- **No service interruptions**

- **Self-Healing**

- **Scalable**

the name of the game, so Microsoft has answered the call with IIS 6.0. Thanks to a complete re-architecture, IIS 6.0 provides a stable platform for web application hosting.

IIS 6.0 was designed to support the following goals:

- Isolation – IIS 6.0 supports an application model where each website runs in an environment isolated from other websites as well as from the core web server code.
- No service interruptions – IIS 6.0 greatly reduces the need for reboots. Even restarting the web service is now rarely needed. If a website fails, it can be restarted without causing an interruption to any of the other websites hosted on the server.
- Self-Healing – Crashed websites can be automatically restarted. If the website experiences a memory leak due to bad code, the website with the faulty code will periodically be restarted automatically.
- Scalable – IIS 6.0 fully supports both scale out and scale up models. It also provides support for NLBS, and Application Center. IIS 6.0 can support several thousand websites on a single server.

IIS 6.0 provides a dynamic hosting environment that automatically detects memory leaks, access violations, code errors, and knows the appropriate response for each of these events. IIS 6.0 introduces the concept of Worker Process Isolation. In Worker Process Isolation mode the kernel handles queuing, application isolation and process management. This ensures prompt corrective action and, if necessary, containment of rogue code or similar errors.

We wanted to make sure that IIS stays up and running all the time. And if for any reason an application hosted on IIS goes down, it doesn't take the web server with it.

—Jeff Kercher

IIS 6 Program Manager, Microsoft Corporation

Architecture

The IIS 6.0 re-architecture completely isolates web applications from affecting the functionality of the system. IIS 6.0 is divided in three components:
1. Http.sys, the HTTP listener.
2. The Web-Processing Core, which manages authentication, authorization and the loading of ISAPI filters.
3. Web Administration Service (WAS), which handles configuration and process management.

Http.sys Listener

Http.sys is a device driver that listens for and queues requests for every website hosted on an instance of IIS 6.0. Http.sys routes these requests to their respective application pools. Each website has its own separate application pool. Developer code runs in a dedicated application pool, not under Http.sys.

In addition, each application pool is isolated from every other application pool on the server. This protection and isolation ensures that bad code on one website will not affect the operation of any other site, or effect the Http.sys process itself. If a website's application pool crashes, Http.sys reacts by attempting to start a new application pool for the website. This often enables automatic recovery from many errors that were fatal in IIS 5.0. Http.sys is compatible with both IPv4 and IPv6 protocols.

Web Processing Core and Worker Process Isolation

The Web Processing Core, which runs as the W3wp.exe process, handles authentication and authorization, and is responsible for the worker process isolation mode. The Web processing Core receives requests from Http.sys and also handles requests for static web pages, ASP, ISAPI extensions, and CGI scripts.

Worker Process Isolation mode insures that **all** application code is run in an isolated environment. It is designed so that this mandatory code isolation requires very little performance overhead. Worker Process Isolation mode eliminates the concept of in-process applications, thereby keeping one malfunctioning website from affecting other websites on the server. This enhancement also allows for true CPU throttling, which is built into the IIS 6.0 Microsoft Management Console (MMC). Worker Process Isolation mode simplifies the process of maintaining a stable shared web environment.

Web Administration Service

Like HTTP.sys, WAS is isolated from developer code and therefore has greater stability. WAS is part of svchost.exe and part of the w3service. When IIS 6.0 starts, WAS reads the metabase, starts and configures Http.sys, and manages namespace routing. WAS is responsible for initialing and restarting failed worker processes. WAS works closely with HTTP.sys and w3wp.exe to insure website availability.

Figure 2.1 shows the communications path for requests in IIS 6.0. Http.sys receives the initial request and directs it to the correct worker process. If the worker process is not started, or is unresponsive, WAS will start a new worker process to handle the request. Note that each worker process is separated into application pools, which are discussed in detail in the next section.

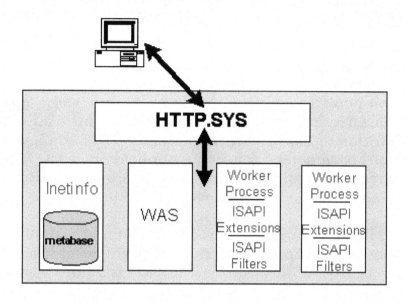

Figure 2.1: IIS 6.0 communications Path

IIS 6.0 Features

Application Pooling

Each application pool runs its own worker process. It is possible to configure multiple web applications in a single application pool. Application development teams should be responsible for determining how application pools are to be assigned.

Conversely, application pools can be assigned several worker processes to service requests, creating what Microsoft refers to as a *Web Garden*. In a Web garden, if one worker process is busy or unable to respond to a request, the request can be routed to another worker process in the application pool.

Not only does IIS 6.0 allow for multiple application pools to ensure that issues on one website do not affect other websites, it also allows the administrator to set an entirely unique set of configuration parameters for each application pool. This gives administrators and developers the flexibility needed to run a shared web environment.

IIS 6.0 supports processor affinity, which is binding an application pool to a single processor. Processor affinity can be used to distribute system resources on a shared server by allowing one server to run four different websites, each bound to a different processor.

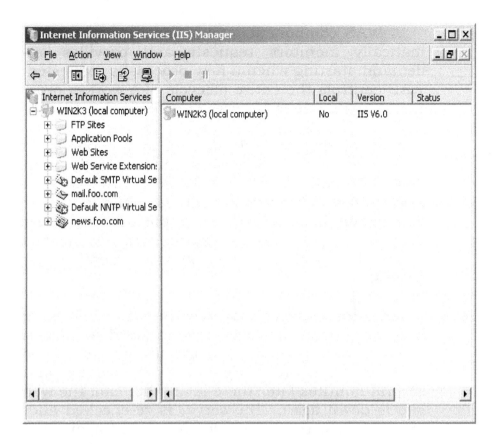

Figure 2.2: Application pools provide flexibility

Automated Recovery

A major issue with IIS 5.0 and earlier versions was the need for continual babysitting. Web servers with frequently changing code needed to be closely monitored because a single error could bring down multiple websites. IIS 6.0 provides automated recovery to help ensure errors are isolated and addressed as they occur without causing major issues on other websites.

A WAS component application manager, automatically monitors requests and provides on-demand starting when a new process is requested. WAS controls the entire lifecycle of a worker process, ensuring the resources are efficiently utilized.

Part of this lifecycle control is the option to have idle worker processes automatically shut down. The idle timeout can be set by the systems integrator or administrator and is configurable per application pool. When the application manager detects a request from a website with an inactive application pool, it simply starts a new worker process.

An administrator may receive a call informing him that one of their web servers are down. Upon investigation, he finds that the IIS service on the web server has failed. He restarts the service, and several minutes later there is another call: the web site is down again. The server is re-checked and, sure enough, the IIS service has failed again and needs to be restarted, a second time. After going through 2 or 3 iterations of this it is realized that the problem is with the code on one of the servers websites. Under IIS 5.0 there was no easy way around this problem. The only way to track down the source of the problem was by trial and error. With IIS 6.0 this problem is eliminated. Not only do isolated application pools protect websites from one another, rapid-fail protection prevents a server from repeatedly restarting a worker process that immediately fails each time it is restarted. Even with separate application pools, continual pounding from a bouncing website can still lead to server problems. IIS 6.0's rapid-fail protection eliminates this possibility.

Health Monitoring

The WAS process monitors each worker process. If one worker process stops responding, WAS stops it and starts up a replacement worker process. If WAS detects a rapid series of restarts and failures, it can place the website in Out Of Service mode. Users will receive a customizable website unavailable error (503 Service Unavailable) when they attempt to access a website placed out of service. Just like most of the other new features of IIS 6.0, rapid-fail protection is easily customized for each application pool and can be turned off if desired.

Worker Process Management

IIS 6.0 not only identifies and corrects issues with worker processes, it also allows for detailed configuration of worker processes to enable advanced management and troubleshooting. This gives engineers the flexibility to design system architecture to meet even the most demanding customer's needs.

Under IIS 5.0 administrators were often required to restart or reboot web servers to address code and application errors, memory leaks, and other anomalies. With IIS 6.0 worker processes can be configured to behave intelligently, based on an application's needs. Worker processes can be configured to recycle based on:

- A predefined schedule

- Time since last recycle
- Number of requests processed
- An unresponsive or delayed ping reply
- Virtual memory usage (to correct memory leaks)

When a worker process is recycled, WAS normally creates a new worker process to handle incoming requests and also drains the current worker process before terminating it. Starting a new worker process and draining the old allows the website to continue to service requests without any service interruption.

At times it may be desirable to leave the troubled or non-responsive worker process running. An example would be when debugging is going to be performed on the worker process. To facilitate this, IIS 6.0 can be configured to start a new worker process all new requests can be forwarded to, leaving the troubled worker process running for later debugging.

Security

Because of the large number of security vulnerabilities that have occurred with IIS 5.0, Microsoft has spent considerable effort in securing IIS 6.0. Process Isolation, IIS lockdown wizard, and tight security controls are just a few of the improvements that Microsoft has integrated into this latest version. The application model used in IIS 5.0 and earlier versions made them difficult to properly secure. Thanks to the complete redesign of IIS 6.0, security was built into the foundation of the IIS 6.0 architecture.

Application Isolation

As discussed earlier, with IIS 6.0 websites run completely isolated from each other. Besides helping to protect websites from faulty code, this isolation also helps create a secure application environment. Microsoft goes as far as to say that IIS 6.0 provides an environment to host even the fiercest competitors on one Web server, implying that the competitors would be unable to hack into each other's sites.

IIS Lockdown Wizard

IIS 6.0 includes a security lockdown wizard that simplifies the task of securing a Web server. Using this wizard, administrators can disable or enable IIS functionality as needed. This allows each web server to be configured with custom levels of functionality based on the type of content they deliver. It should be noted that this latest version of IIS comes pre-configured with the most restrictive permissions in place, allowing only static web pages to be served. If ASP pages, CGI scripts, or other dynamic content is to be served then the lockdown wizard should be used to enable this functionality on the server.

SSL Optimization

Microsoft's IIS 5.0 already has excellent Secure Socket Layer (SSL) performance. IIS 6.0 has improved upon this performance even more by fine-tuning performance enhancements in its SSL implementation. These improvements should place IIS 6.0 squarely in the lead for SSL performance. IIS also allows SSL certificates to be remotely managed, through the use of 'CertObjects'. SSL processing can easily be offloaded to hardware SSL accelerator cards with the use of IIS 6.0's Crypto API provider. The Crypto API provider makes it easy to integrate third-party SSL accelerators with IIS 6.0. Itanium 2 servers excel at the CPU-intensive requests the SSL transactions require. The total cost of ownership for hardware-based solutions should be compared to that of using Itanium 2 servers as an SSL solution.

IIS 6.0 includes many additional improvements to enhance security. These enhancements include a complete rewrite of the FTP (File Transfer Protocol) module, that not only provides increased security, but also allows greater flexibility. Also, IIS 6.0 runs worker processes with very limited access rights. Limited rights prevent widespread abuse of the system in the event that the IIS service account is compromised. Microsoft has made security a priority in all of its .Net products. Nowhere is this more evident than in IIS 6.0.

XML Metabase

In IIS 5.0 metabase corruption was a major problem. The IIS metabase maintains website configuration and settings for every website on the server. If the metabase became corrupt or was lost, it was almost impossible to recover. The IIS 5.0 metabase also made editing web configuration entries very difficult.

In keeping with Microsoft's vision of XML as a universal communications standard, IIS 6.0 uses XML to store all its metadata. XML is more flexible and easier to work with than the binary file that IIS 5.0 uses. With the XML metabase it becomes much easier to backup and restore the metabase. It is much easier to edit or to repair a corrupt database, because the metabase follows a predefined standard. Editing can even be done with MS Notepad, or any other text editor. This standardization also enables exporting and interfacing with the metadata from other applications.

XML Metabase Features

- **Simplified backup and restores**

- **Recovery from Metabase corruption**

- **Flexible Metabase exporting**

- **Improved scalability and performance**

The XML metabase provides a decreased footprint and faster read access, making the startup progress for IIS 6.0 quicker than its predecessors. Additionally, the IIS metabase provides automatic versioning and history. When changes are made to the metabase, IIS creates a backup of the old version and saves it with a unique version ID. This feature provides fast recovery if the metabase becomes corrupted. The metabase can even be edited while running, with no need to stop the IIS service.

Finally, with Admin Base Objects (ABO) Microsoft has simplified importing and exporting of the metabase to different servers, regardless of their operating environment. ABO allows for export or import to an entire tree of servers, merging of configurations, and password protecting of its metadata.

IIS 5 Isolation Mode

Because IIS 6.0 has been completely rewritten to improve reliability and ensure application isolation, in some cases it may not be compatible with web applications written for IIS 5.0, such as web applications that maintain in-process persistence session state. IIS 6.0 addresses this potential conflict by offering an IIS 5.0 isolation mode. This mode offers backward compatibility for any web applications that are not compatible with IIS 6.0's isolation mode. This alterative isolation mode offers some of the performance improvements of IIS 6.0, but by default runs applications in a shared space, like IIS 5.0. Additionally, the application pool options that exist in IIS 5.0—low, medium and high—can also be used in IIS 6.0, by using the IIS 5.0 isolation mode. This backwards compatibility helps in the smooth transition from IIS version 5.0 to 6.0.

Architectural Examples

Web Farms

Web farms are groups of web servers that work together to deliver content for one or more sites. IIS 6.0 can be used with NLBS or Application Center to allow the creation of web farms that provide both failover and load balancing. Creating a web farm on IIS 6.0 has significant advantages over other hosting platforms due to its complete application isolation. It also has the ability to run literally tens of thousands of websites from a web farm, thanks to its XML metabase.

Internet Service Providers

IIS 6.0's application isolation enables IIS to compete with Apache in the Internet Service Provider (ISP) arena. IIS 6.0 can be used for high volume website hosting, because a code error on one website will no longer result in the possible disruption of services to every other site on the server. Customers can be given the ability to write their own APS and CGI scripts. IIS 6.0 can support the hosting of several thousand different websites all hosted on a single server.

Isolated COM+ Server

When hosting multiple CPU-intensive COM+ objects, it is often advisable to have them housed on a dedicated server. When utilizing CPU-intensive COM+ objects, Itanium servers can be implemented to handle the heavy workload. Furthermore, some COM+ objects can be manipulated to gain unauthorized access to the server or network. To prevent possible security breaches, COM+ objects are often placed behind a firewall. Figure 2.3 shows just such a configuration.

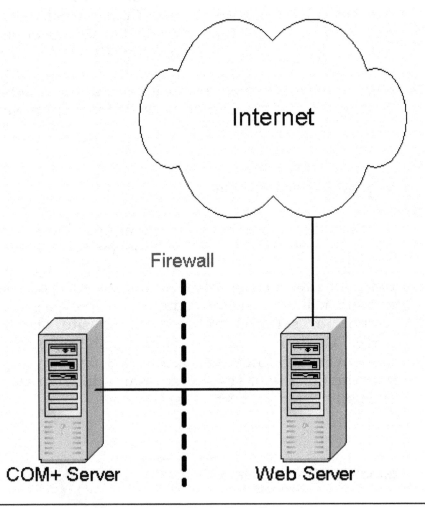

Figure 2.3: Com+ server isolated behind a firewall

Websites with Database Access

E-commerce websites often utilize a backend database to assist with transactions such as inventory lookup, customer information, and order processing. For failover and load balancing, multiple web servers may be accessing a single database server for data retrieval.

Depending on the network configuration, the web server or servers may be in front of or behind the firewall. For security, the database server should be placed behind the firewall, and should be configured to accept connections using a nonstandard port. Some networks place web servers in front of the firewall, under the premise that if a web server is hacked, access to the entire network will not be compromised. While this may prevent a compromise of your entire network, it makes your web servers much more susceptible to attack. It is therefore recommended that even if your web servers are not behind the primary firewall, they should be placed behind a secondary firewall, or Packet filtering device, to create an additional firebreak. (See Figure 2.4.)

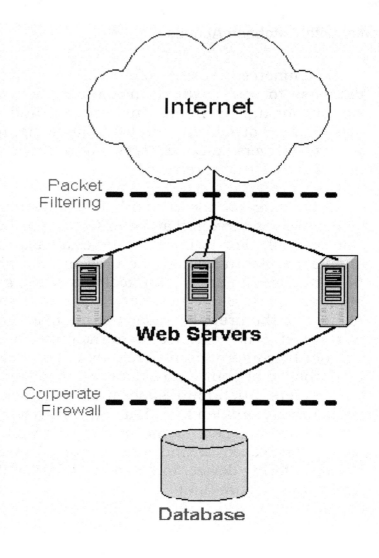

Figure 2.4: Web servers with database backend

Summary

IIS 6.0 is a major step in the evolution of Microsoft's web services. Many of its new features

are designed to address common issues with previous versions of IIS. By far, the most substantial
new IIS feature is the complete redesign of the application architecture that ensures all application
code is run in a fully isolated environment. If
properly utilized, IIS 6.0 can provide flexible, secure, and dependable web hosting for an enterprise of any size.

Chapter 3

Windows Server 2003

Microsoft Windows Server 2003 is not a major system upgrade. Windows Server 2003 simply brings enhancements to the Windows server family. That is not to mitigate the advances Windows Server 2003 offers. Windows Server 2003 has built-in support for the .Net framework, XML, ASP .Net and IIS 6.0. Some of these features can be added on to Windows Server 2000 to some limited extent, but without the same functionality.

For example, in Windows Server 2000, IIS 5.0 can be upgraded to IIS 5.1, which provides some of the same features and compatibility with

ASP.Net that IIS 6.0 provides. IIS 5.1 basically just adds these features on to the existing IIS 5.0 code base. IIS 6.0, on the other hand, has been re-written from the ground up to provide scalability, security, and—above all—stability.

Windows Server 2003 Advances

There are four different versions of Windows 2003 (five if you count Windows XP). These are:
1. Standard Edition
2. Enterprise Edition
3. Datacenter Edition
4. Web edition.

This chapter focuses on Windows Server 2003 Enterprise Edition, as it is not only commonly used in Enterprise Networks, but also has the balance of features commonly used in web servers.

Powerful Performance

Windows Server 2003 Enterprise Edition supports up to eight 32-bit CPUs per server, with eight-way symmetric multiprocessing (SMP). This allows for increased server performance and improved scale-up. The Itanium 64-bit version supports up to sixty-four processors in a single system via SMP.

Windows clustering has been expanded with the introduction of eight-node clustering with advanced clustering configuration options. Memory capacity has been dramatically increased, now allowing 32 gigabytes of memory in the Windows 32-bit version and 512 gigabytes in the Itanium version. This opens up new possibilities, such as allowing an entire database to reside in memory.

Simplified Management and Deployment

Windows Server 2003 has made several improvements to Active Directory, making it more versatile, and dependable to use. Specifically, Active Directory in Windows Server 2003 provides:

- Easier deployment and management.
- Greater security.
- Improved performance and dependability.

Active Directory Management

Windows Server 2003 makes it easier for administrators to manage and configure the Active Directory. Improved tools for migration and management simplify the operations of large enterprises. Improved management tools offer drag-and-drop capabilities, multiple object selection, and query re-use. Active Directory management is enhanced with improved group policies and the ability to rename Active Directory domains.

The Active Directory Migration Tool (ADMT) version 2.0 allows administrators to migrate passwords from Windows NT 4.0 or 2000 to Windows Server 2003 domains. Group policy is simplified with the Microsoft Group Policy Management Console (GPMC). New functionality includes:

- The ability to manage multiple domains.
- Backup and restore abilities.
- Group Policy object (GPO) reporting.

Large enterprise networks benefit from the flexibility to use cross-forest trusts. Cross-forest trusts allow users to access resources in other forests without having to re-supply a username and password. This trust is managed using Kerberos or NTML. This allows different organizations in a single company to have multiple forests, but still preserve the benefits of Active Directory.

Software restriction policies allow administrators to protect their network from unknown or suspicious software by restricting what software is allowed to run. Software Restriction policies reduce the number of software mis-configuration and support calls while maintaining a consistent computing environment. This policy is flexible enough to allow exception rules to be created on a case-by-case basis if desired.

Microsoft has focused on increasing dependability throughout the server environment. Key features are health monitoring, which verifies replication between Domain Controllers, and Inter-Site Topology Generator (ISTG) that provides support for larger forests than Windows 2000, providing increased scalability.

Security in Windows Server 2003

Faced with harsh criticism of their Windows platform Microsoft has made security a major focus for Windows Server 2003.

Bugs and security holes are a major cause of concern for IT professionals and managers alike.

In an effort to help address these concerns, Microsoft has included Common Language Runtime software in its latest release of Windows Server. Common Language Runtime software ensures that applications run without errors and checks for the correct security permissions, ensuring that programs only perform allowed operations. This should result in less vulnerability for trojans and malicious hackers to exploit. Common Language Runtime software checks for where the code was downloaded or installed, whether it has a digital signature from a trusted developer, and whether the code has been altered since it was digitally signed.

Trustworthy Computing

To address viruses and trojans that infect software applications and components, Microsoft has made Trustworthy Computing a key focus for Windows Server 2003. Trustworthy Computing is a framework for developing devices and software to help ensure that they are equally secure and trustworthy. Trustworthy Computing requires other vendors to support Microsoft's implementation. By re-designing Windows Server security, Microsoft has taken the first step toward making Trustworthy Computing a reality.

Encrypting File System

To address file level security Microsoft has included an encrypting file system in Windows Server 2003. Microsoft's Encrypting File System is built into NTFS and verifies users based on the token created when they log on. This ensures that only the user who encrypts a file can open and work with it.

Table 3.1 displays a list of additional Security features Microsoft has build into Windows Server 2003.

Internet Connection Firewall	A software-based firewall protects Windows Server 2003 server computers connected directly to the internet.
Secure IAS Server	Internet Authentication Server maintains secure logins for Dialup, VPN, and extranet users.
Software Restriction Policies	System administrator can now set the policy for software installation, allowing only approved software to be installed.
Web Security	IIS security has been improved with a complete redesign and a default locked down installation.
Offline File Database Encryption	Windows Server 2003 now provides the ability to encrypt the offline file database.
FIPS-compliant Kernel-mode Crypto Module	The cryptographic module runs as a driver in Kernel-mode and uses Federal Information Processing Standards (FIPS) algorithms for Enhanced security.
Digest Security Package	IIS 6.0 and Active Directory both support the digest security package, based on RFC 2617 and RFC 2222.
SSL improvements	Secure Sockets Layer (SSL) performance has been increased by over 35 percent.
Credential Manager	Provides a secure store for user credentials. This provides a single secure sign-on for roaming users.
SSL Authentication Enhancement	SSL session cache is cached by multiple processes reducing the times that users have to re-authenticate.

Table 3.1 Windows Server 2003 Security Features

Clustering in Windows 2003

Microsoft has improved and expanded clustering in Windows Server 2003. Windows Server 2003 Enterprise edition supports up to eight-way clusters. This provides scalability and high availability for various applications including MS SQL, Exchange, file and print servers, as well as other application servers. In Microsoft Clustering Services (MSCS) if one member of a cluster fails, or is taken offline for maintenance, another cluster member takes over all service requests.

Windows Server 2003 supports geographically disperse clusters, thereby allowing for greater flexibility in designing high availability solutions. Additionally, Microsoft has added the ability to support N+I cluster configurations (N active with I spare). N+I clusters allow one server to act as failover for several primary servers. This will greatly reduce the number of servers required to maintain high availability applications.

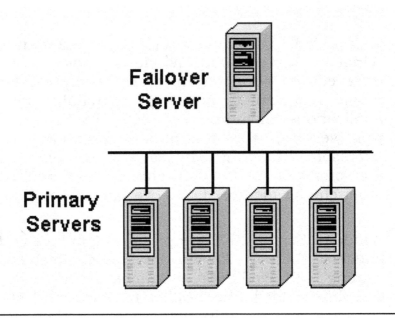

Figure 3.1: Example of a N+I Cluster

XML Web Services

Microsoft has built-in XML support into the core of Windows server 2003. XML gives systems a simple and standardized communications medium, regardless of their platform or programming language. Microsoft has integrated XML with SOAP and UDDI to provide XML Web Services, enabling different client applications to communicate using a universal communications medium.

SOAP enables applications or services to make and process requests made from other applications and services. The UDDI service is a central directory, enabling systems all over the Internet to discover and then communicate using XML

Microsoft SharePoint Server

Microsoft's SharePoint server does just what its name implies: it is a point or place to share virtually any online information. SharePoint is divided into two products:

1. SharePoint Team Services, primarily for small organizations with a small group of users
2. SharePoint Portal Server, Microsoft's enterprise class solution.

SharePoint Team Services licensing is included with Windows Server 2003, while SharePoint Portal Server requires additional licensing to be purchased.

	Team Services	Portal Server
Number of users	5-75	75+
Services	Discussions, Notifications, Surveys	Discussions, Notifications
Customization	Browser-based, FrontPage, SDK	Web Parts, SDK
Document Management	Publish	Check-in and out, Versioning, Routing, Publishing,
Client Applications	Browser, MS Office, FrontPage	Browser, MS Office, Windows Explorer
Storage	MS SQL Server	Web Storage System
Licensing	Included in Windows Server 2003	Server and Client Licensing required

Table 3.2 SharePoint Product Comparison

Team Services

SharePoint Team Services is designed for online collaboration and information sharing. It allows users to engage in online discussions and surveys, publish documents, and post announcements. Companies often assign each team or individual organization a Team Services site to be customized and maintained by the group's members.

SharePoint Team Services provides easy customization using a web-based front-end, that allows even novice users to customize a Team Services website. While advanced users can use MS FrontPage, or even a Software Developer's Kit (SDK), Microsoft recommends Team Services for groups with 75 or fewer active participants.

Portal Server

SharePoint Portal Server includes most of the functionality of SharePoint Team Services, with enhancements designed to meet the requirements of large enterprise organizations. One of the major enhancements provided in SharePoint Services is its Document Management functionality, which provides document checkout, versioning, routing and publishing capabilities. Portal Server allows for enterprise-wide searching.

Summary

The complete list of enhancements Microsoft has made to Windows Server 2003 is too extensive to fully cover in this chapter. Microsoft has focused on increasing security of its core code base, as well as adding new features to enhance security. Windows Server 2003 allows for flexible and robust clusters. XML support has been built into the core operating system. These improvements help to make Windows Server 2003 an ideal platform for running a complete web application solution.

Chapter 4

Internet Information Server 6.0 Installation

To help Windows Server 2003 maintain a secure environment, IIS 6.0 is not installed by default. The installation of IIS 6.0 in Windows Server 2003 is very similar to the installation of IIS 5.0 in Windows Server 2000. This chapter covers the actual installation of IIS 6.0, while the next chapter details the basic configuration and common options configured in IIS 6.0. This chapter provides just enough detail to get a Windows Server 2003 completely installed and running with IIS 6.0. More specific information about the new features of IIS 6.0 can be found in chapter 5, *Application and Website Configuration.*

Getting Started

Like IIS 5.0 in Windows Server 2000, IIS 6.0 on Windows Server 2003 is installed by selecting **Add/Remove Windows Components** under the **Add or Remove Programs** option of the Control Panel.

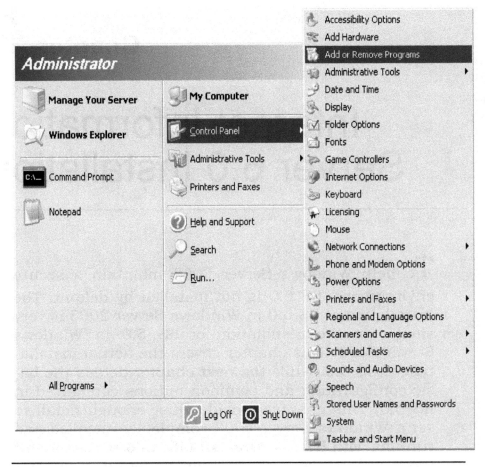

Figure 4.1: Location of Add or Remove Programs

Installing IIS 6.0

Different from Windows Server 2000, the actual option for installing IIS is now buried under **Components, Application Server** (Figure 4.2). This is the same location where ASP.Net and COM+/DTC network access support are installed. Click on the **Add or Remove Programs** option to continue with the installation.

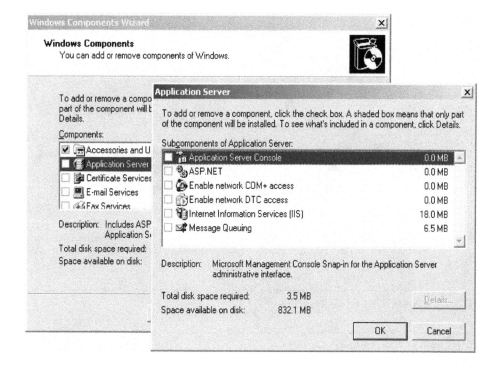

Figure 4.2: Windows Components Dialog Box

Checking **Internet Information Services (IIS)** and then clicking **Details** allows the user to select what IIS 6.0 options to install. Some of the components have sub-components that can be selected or deselected by clicking **Details**. These options are described at length in Table 4.1.

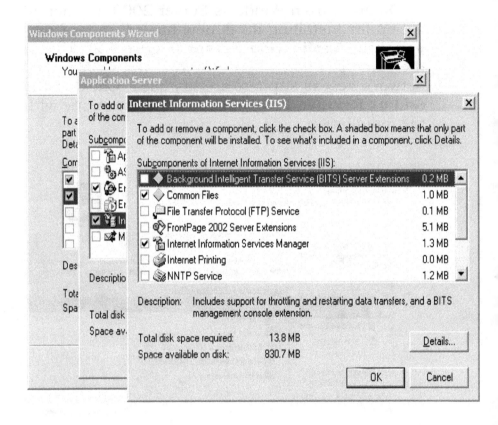

Figure 4.3: IIS Install Options

BITS Server Extensions

The Background Intelligent Transfer Service (BITS), known as a *drizzle service*, is responsible for background file transfers and queue manager management. BITS throttles file requests to maximize bandwidth utilization and improve the end-user experience. BITS works with IIS to maintain web server quality of service.
Details to enable the following BITS Server components:

> **BITS Server Extensions ISAPI**: This option allows IIS to drizzle requests with the help of the BITS server.

BITS Server Extensions Snap-in: Enable this option to access and view the BITS graphical user interface (GUI).

Common Files

Although the common files are required, some of the subcomponents can be deselected.

File Transfer Protocol (FTP) Server

The File Transfer Protocol (FTP) allows the sharing of files over the Internet via TCP/IP. Making files available via FTP is often preferable to using HTTP as the FTP is more robust.

FrontPage 2002 Server Extensions

FrontPage 2002 Server Extensions enable the viewing and management of a website in a graphical user interface using FrontPage as the authoring tool. FrontPage allows easy creation of Web sites as well as a simplified interface for web pages management. While a website is being edited, FrontPage keeps a connection open to IIS, saving and changing the web files on the fly. Microsoft Clustering does not support Microsoft FrontPage Server Extensions.

Internet Information Services Manager

The IIS Manager is a graphical user interface that is used to administer all websites on a server. The IIS Manager replaces the Internet Service Manager used in IIS 5.0. Without IIS Manager, IIS can only be managed via coded scripts that rely on the IIS APIs to create sites, applications, virtual directories, and change settings.

NNTP Service

The Network News Transfer Protocol (NNTP) manages network news messages to NNTP servers and to NNTP newsreader clients. NNTP stores news articles in a central database, allowing users to determine which articles to read. Various options include indexing, cross-referencing, and expiration of aged messages.

If NNTP is installed, the NNTP Service help file can be accessed by browsing to **file:\\%systemroot%\help\news.chm** in your Internet browser.

SMTP Service

Simple Mail Transfer Protocol (SMTP) is used to set up an intranet mail service that works hand in hand with IIS. SMTP is a TCP/IP-based service for sending e-mail messages over the Internet. This protocol can also be used to route messages over the network.

If SMTP is installed, the SMTP service help file can be accessed by browsing to **file:\\%systemroot%\help\mail.chm** in your Internet browser.

World Wide Web Publishing Service

The World Wide Web Publishing Service is the component that IIS uses to serve WebPages over HTTP. The World Wide Web Publishing Service must be installed for IIS server WebPages. If this option is not selected IIS will be disabled.

Subcomponents of the World Wide Web Publishing Service (WWW service) include:

Active Server Pages – Required to use ASP on the web server. If this option is not selected, .asp requests will not function properly, returning a 404 error.

Internet Data Connector - Required to use the Internet Data Connection. If this option is not selected, .idc requests will not function properly, returning a 404 error.

Remote Administration (HTML) - Enables remote Web administration of an IIS Web server from any Web browser on the network (or over the Internet).

Remote Desktop Web Connection: Enables connectivity to a computer's desktop from a remote location and runs applications as if they were being run from the console.

Server-Side Includes - Allows server-side include (SSI) files on the web server. If this option is not selected, .shtm, .shtml, and .stm requests will return a 404 error.

WebDav Publishing - Enables Web Distributed Authoring and Versioning (WebDAV). WebDAV works similar to File Transfer Protocol. However, while WebDav is more flexible than FTP, it is also less secure.

Web Site Administration – Allows for local administration of the web server. If this option is not selected, IIS does not run on your server.

Table 4.1: IIS 6.0 Component Options

After selecting the subcomponent, click **OK**, then **OK** again, and finally click **Next**. The system will respond by beginning the installation process. Figure 4.4 shows the Install Wizard process window that indicates the installation progress.

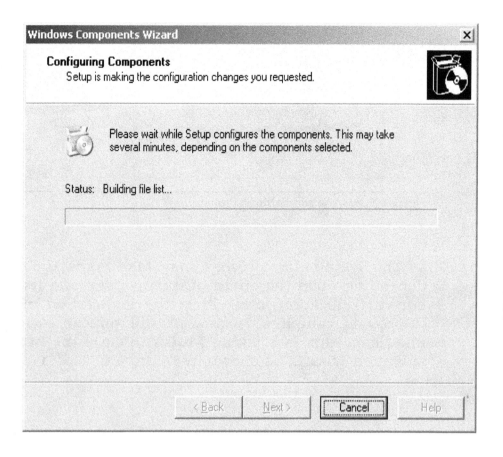

Figure 4.4: Installation Process Window

At any time during the installation the system may prompt you for the Windows Server 2003 CD-ROM. Inserting the CD-ROM into the system's CD-ROM drive, will make the system automatically recognize it and continue the installation. Alternatively, the wizard can be pointed to a local or networked copy of the system files.

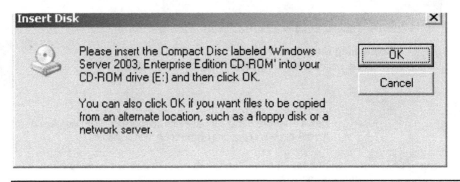

Figure 4.5: Insert Windows Media Prompt

The installation process may take some time depending upon the speed of the machine and its current utilization level. Once the installation of IIS 6.0 is complete, a prompt will appear. Acknowledge this by clicking **Finish** to close the Installation Wizard, as shown in Figure 4.6.

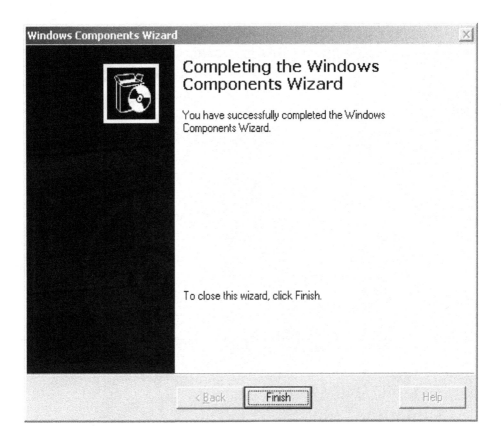

Figure 4.6: Install Wizard – Installation Complete

The system may then briefly display a Windows Setup screen with a Please wait message (Figure 4.7). Once this screen disappears, setup is complete. Under Windows Server 2003 there is no need to reboot the server when IIS 6.0 is installed or when components are added or removed.

Figure 4.7: Final Setup Window

Summary

In Windows Server 2003 IIS 6.0 must be added after the initial system build; it is not installed as part of the default build. The installation procedure for IIS 6.0 in Windows Server 2003 is much the same as the installation of IIS 5.0 in Windows Server 2000.

IIS 6.0 is installed via the **Add/Remove Windows Components** window, under the **Application Server** selection. The Windows Component Install Wizard walks administrators through the installation process. Installing IIS 6.0 on Windows 2003 does not require a reboot.

Chapter 5

Application and Website Configuration

To address security concerns, Microsoft has configured IIS 6.0 so that after installation IIS is only able to serve static HTML pages. Unlike previous versions, IIS 6.0 is installed in a somewhat locked down state. This means that if a website is using any custom components, such as ASP or server-side includes (SSI), you will need to configure IIS to allow these components to function properly. This chapter will review the process for setting up and running a website using the IIS Services Manager, the replacement for the IIS 5.0 MMC console. This chapter will also address common features that Microsoft did not lockdown, which might cause security issues.

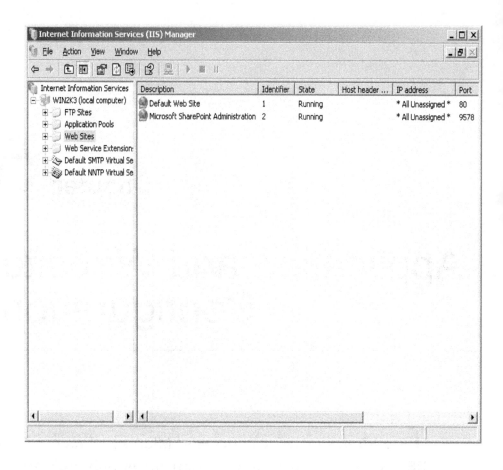

Figure 5.1: IIS Manager

Getting Started

The IIS 6.0 Services Manager looks similar to the MMC snap-in used to manage previous versions of IIS (Figure 5.1). The Microsoft SharePoint Administration site is installed and running by default. Although Microsoft has shown a major focus on security with this latest release, FTP, NNTP, and SMTP services are also all enabled and running by default.

Locking Down IIS

Stopping these services though the IIS Services Manager will allow them to automatically restart the next time the computer is rebooted, potentially compromising security. If these services are not required, they should be disabled though the Services window, which in Windows Server 2003 is now located under **Start, Administrative Tools**.

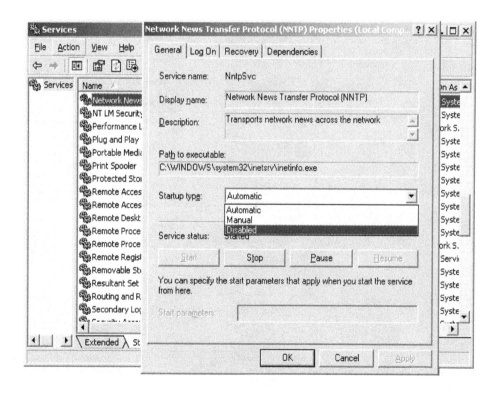

Figure 5.2: NNTP Services Properties

Once all the unused services are disabled, FrontPage Server Extensions 2002 should be addressed. FrontPage Server extensions offer powerful enhancements to IIS, such as embedded search capabilities and database access. These enhancements do come at a cost—decreased security. FrontPage Server Extensions have often been the target of hackers and trojans alike. Unless FrontPage Server extensions are required to support a specific web application, disabling them is highly recommended.

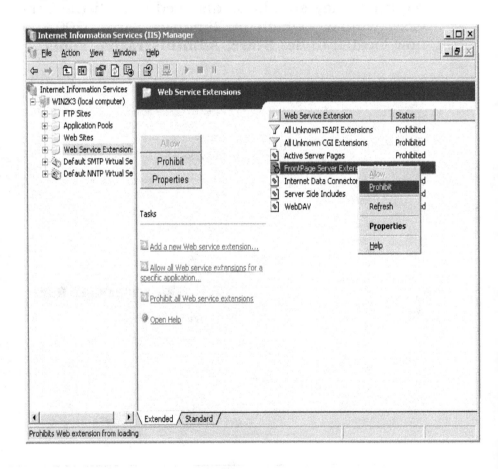

Figure 5.3: Configuring Web Server Extensions

The last step to provide a basic level of security for IIS 6.0 is to stop both the default application pool and the MS SharePoint application pool. Unlike the unwanted services that were disabled in the previous paragraph, these built-in application pools do not need to be disabled.

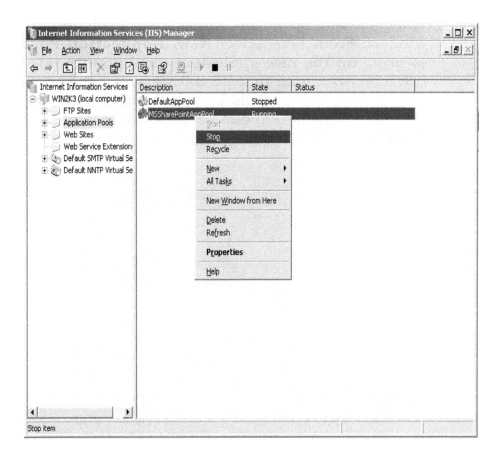

Figure 5.4: Stopping the MS SharePoint Application Pool

Application Pool Configuration

The system is now ready to have its first website configured. Right-clicking the **Application Pools** folder in the left pane of the IIS Services Manager will open the Application Pool options window. From here select **New, Application Pool** to bring up the new application pool prompt (Figure 5.5). Also, note that IIS 6.0 allows for the creation of application pools from a configuration file, if desired. This option can be used to automate the setup of multiple application pools.

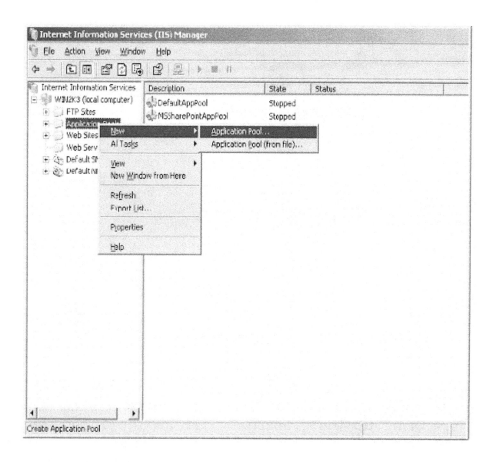

Figure 5.5: Create a New Application Pool

Set the Application pool ID as desired (figure 5.6). Ideally this name should correspond with the name or function of your website or application. Since this is the first custom application pool on this server, use the default settings and then select **OK**. Once an application pool is already set up, its settings can be copied by choosing **Use existing application pool as template** and selecting the desired application pool name.

Add New Application Pool

Application pool ID: | My Website|

Application pool settings

⦿ Use default settings for new application pool

○ Use existing application pool as template

Application pool name: | DefaultAppPool

| OK | Cancel | Help |

Figure 5.6: Configure the Application Pool ID

Application Pool Properties

Right-click on the ID of the newly created application pool and select **Properties**. This will bring up the properties page for the application pool we just created. The properties page is separated into four tabs: **Recycling**, **Performance**, **Health**, and **Identity**.

Recycling

The **Recycling** tab allows each application pool to be configured to restart whenever certain conditions are met. **Recycle worker process (in minutes)** allows the worker process to be restarted after a given number of minutes. Chapter 2 discusses how the worker process controls access to each website. For more information on the worker process, please refer to *Chapter 2, IIS 6.0 Features*.

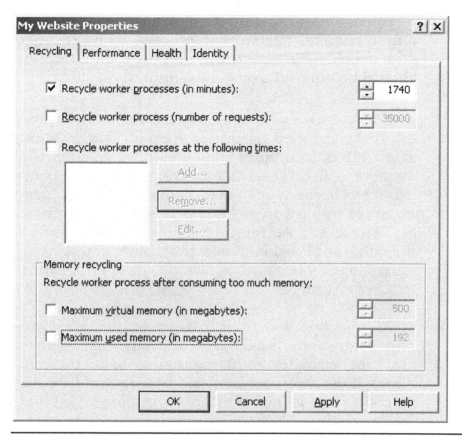

Figure 5.7: Web Site Application Pool Properties - Recycling tab

Recycle worker process (number of requests) allows the application pool's worker process to be recycled after a given number of user requests. Note that each visitor may make numerous requests in any given visit. Therefore, this setting cannot be used to instruct the worker process to restart after a specific number of visitors.

Recycle worker process at the following times provides the ability to recycle the worker process at various times throughout the day. This option does not allow for the worker process to be recycled at a predetermined day in the future. It only allows for the worker process to be recycled at a specific time each day. Times for this option should be entered using a 24-hour style clock.

The last two settings allow for the worker process to be recycled based on memory usage. **Maximum virtual memory** indicates how much virtual memory will be used before the application pool's worker process is restarted, while **Maximum used memory** applies to all memory, virtual and physical. These two setting are primarily used for addressing application pools that have components such as COM+ objects, which develop memory leaks over time.

All the options on the **Recycle** tab allow administrators to proactively address the issue of crashing websites or derogated website performance. These are common issues encountered due to code that is not written or implemented perfectly.

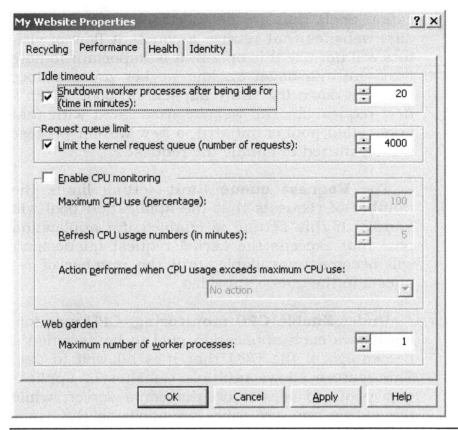

Figure 5.8: Website Application Pool Properties - Performance Tab

Performance

The **Performance** tab (figure 5.8) allows an administrator to set configuration parameters that effect the performance of both individual application pools as well as managing resources shared across the entire server.

Idle timeout gives an administrator the option of shutting down a worker process after it has been idle for a specified number of minutes. This setting can be used to free up resources on application pools that are not used frequently. Generally, websites that receive a constant flow of visitors will not use this option. It is important to note that shutting down an idle worker process does not shut down the entire application pool. When a new request for the website associated with that application pool is initiated, a new worker process will be started to handle the request.

The **Request queue limit** setting limits the number of requests that the application pool will handle. If this setting is enabled, an application pool that exceeds the kernel request queue limit will become unavailable until the number of requests in the queue subsides.

Under **Enable CPU monitoring,** CPU monitoring allows each application pool to be assigned a percentage of the CPU that it is allowed to use. This feature allows multiple websites or application pools to coexist on the same server, while preventing one site from monopolizing the available CPU. The maximum CPU usage percentage access all application pools is not required to equal 100%.

Four websites could be setup with separate application pools, each allowed to utilize 100% of the available CPU. If one or more site's CPU utilization spiked at any given time, the performance of all sites would be affected. Conversely, if each of the four sites had a maximum CPU threshold of 20%, IIS 6.0 would, in theory, only use a maximum of 80% of the CPU's Capacity.

Refresh CPU usage numbers determines the rate at which the CPU utilization is refreshed. The lower the interval, the more accurate the CPU monitoring. However, there is a performance cost associated with frequent refreshing. The default of 5 minutes is an appropriate starting point for most application pools.

If an application pool exceeds the maximum CPU usage, it can be set to shut down. Selecting this option will make the website associated with the application pool unreachable.

A Web garden can be managed by increasing the number of worker processes assigned to a given application pool. Web gardens typically util-ize two or more worker processes.

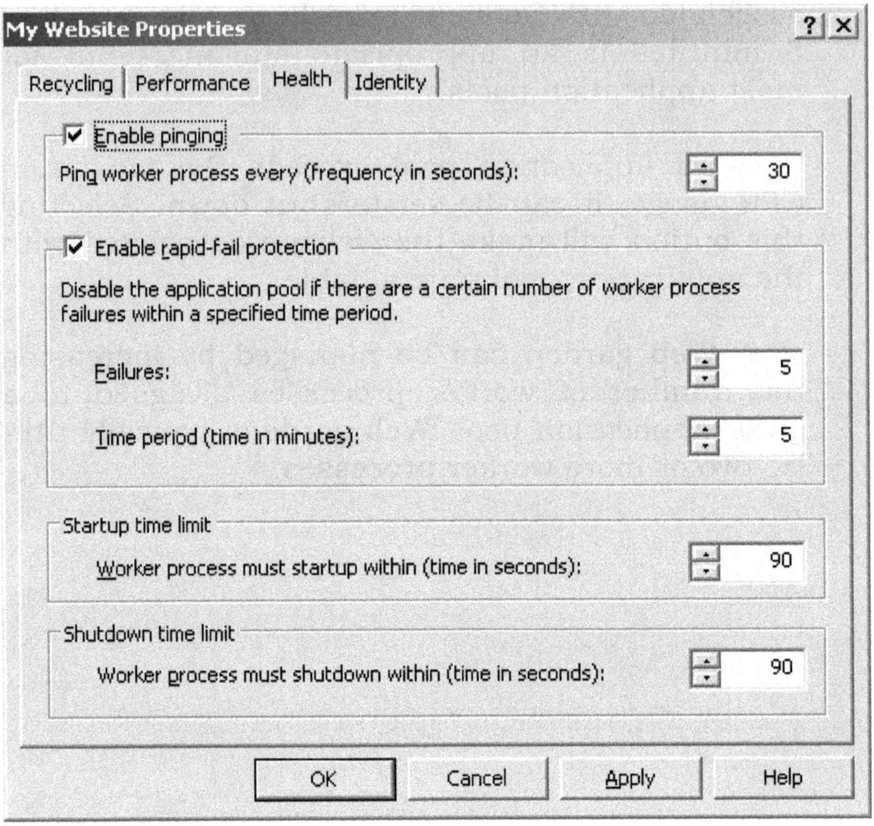

Figure 5.9: Website Application Pool Properties - Health Tab

Health

All application pool health monitoring is configured on the **Health** tab of the application pool
properties, shown in figure 5.9. **Enable pinging**
allows IIS to check the status of the worker process at specified intervals. If the worker process
appears to be hanging, IIS will start a new worker
process and forward all new request to the new
worker process. Disabling pinging completely disables worker process monitoring.

Occasionally, a website fails immediately after being started or restarted. If the system is set to automatically restart this can cause performance derogation, or even a system crash. **Enable Rapid fail protection** is designed to prevent this. It can be configured to respond to the number of failures as well as setting the time intervals.

The **Startup time limit** and **Shutdown time limit**, determine how much time the system spends attempting to start and shut down worker processes. Remember, user requests cannot be processed while a worker process is starting up or shutting down. If a worker process fails to start in the specified time period, IIS will attempt to start another worker process. If rapid fail protection is enabled, this also increments the failure count. If a worker process fails to shut down in the specified time, it is simply left running and a new worker process is started. No further requests will be sent to the non-responsive worker process.

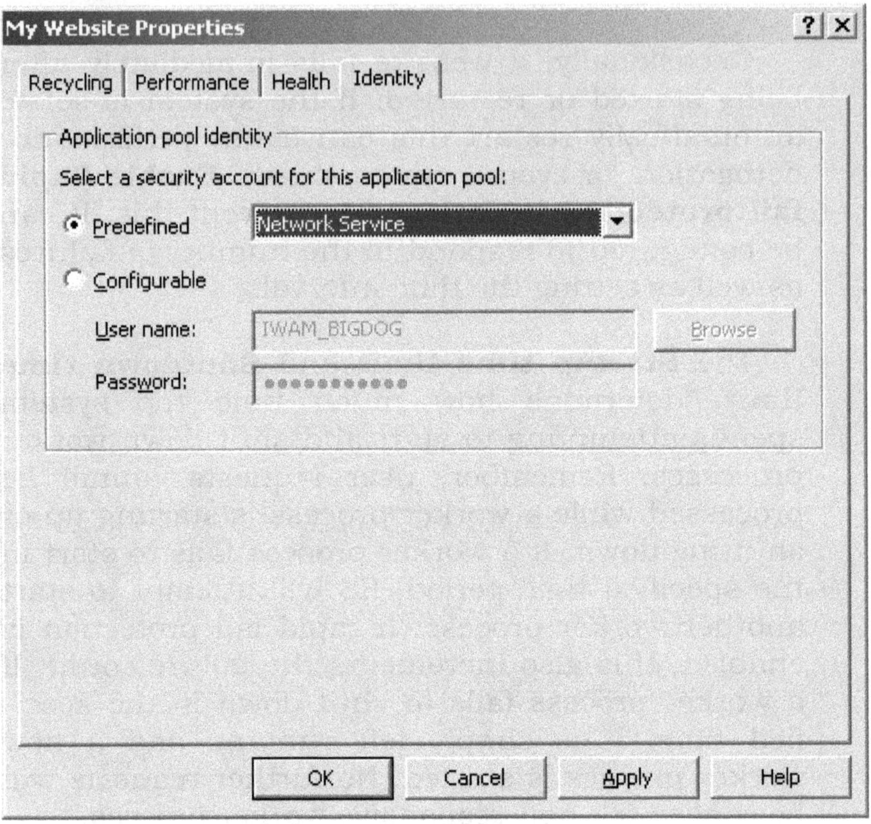

Figure 5.10: Website Application Pool Properties - Identity Tab

Identity

The **Identity** tab, shown in figure 5.10, selects the context under which the application pool runs. This can be one of three selections under the **Predefined** radio button; **Network Service**, **Local Service**, or the **Local System** account. Additionally, any system account can be used by selecting the **Configurable** radio button. Each application pool can have its own identity; that is, each can run under a separate account.

Configuring a Website

Since website properties are configured in much the same way as in IIS 5.0, this section will not address most of the basic configuration options that have remained unchanged. Instead, this section will address the website properties new to IIS 6.0, specifically those that relate to application pools and the new architecture introduced in IIS 6.0. First time IIS users should refer to the appendix for basic website configuration information.

New websites are created using the **New Website Wizard**, just like in the previous version of IIS. Additionally, like application pools, websites can be created from a configuration file. Once a new site is created using either the Wizard or configuration file, the site will need to be started.

Website Properties

As in previous versions of IIS, the website properties are easily accessed by right-clicking the desired website and selecting **Properties**. It is immediately evident that all of the options available in IIS 5.0 are included in IIS 6.0; in fact, most can be found in the same location (Figure 5.11).

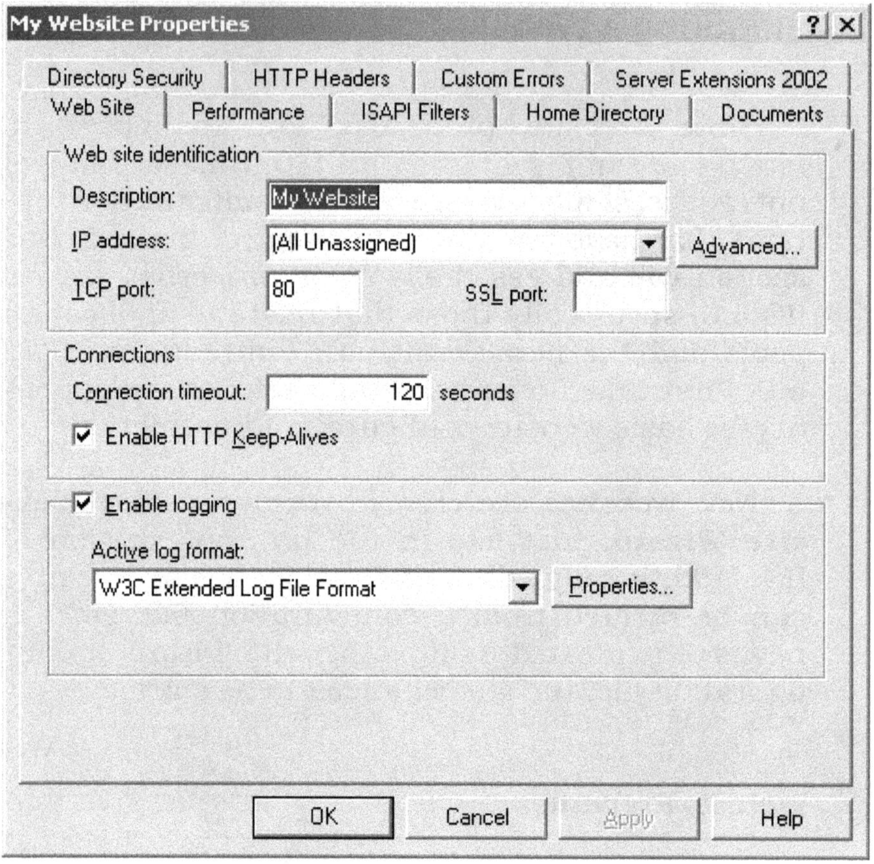

Figure 5.11: Web Site Configuration Properties

Under the **Home Directory** tab, a website can be configured to use a specific application pool. This is accomplished by selecting the desired application pool from the dropdown menu and clicking **Apply** (Figure 5.12). This requires the application pool to have already been created.

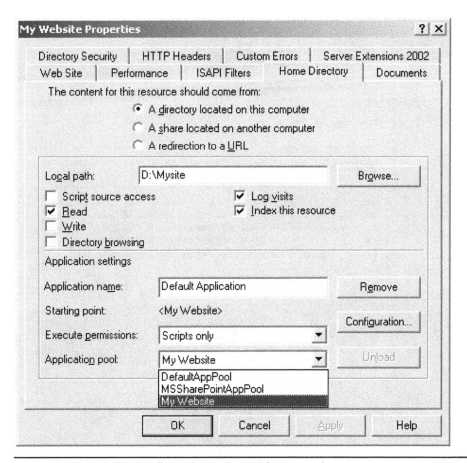

Figure 5.12: Website Configuration - Home Directory tab

Application extensions can be edited by clicking the **Configuration** button. Most common application extensions are included by default. This is another example of how Microsoft's locked down IIS installation still requires some fine-tuning. For security purposes, it is often prudent to remove application extensions that will not be needed.

The most notable change to the **Application Configuration** window is the **Wildcard application maps**. This will allow an application map to be used for any extension that is not already defined, as in Figure 5.13.

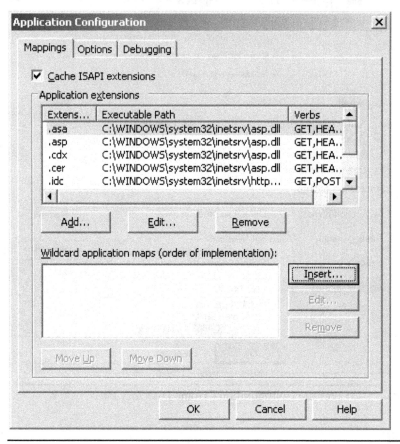

Figure 5.13 Application Configuration Mappings

The **Documents** tab remains unchanged from IIS 5.0. No one should be surprised that Microsoft chose to ignore standard Internet conventions by neglecting to add "index.html" as the default content page. However, many may be surprised to learn that Microsoft failed to add an option to enable a document header. Needless to say, most applications will require that index.html be added as a default content page (Figure 5.14).

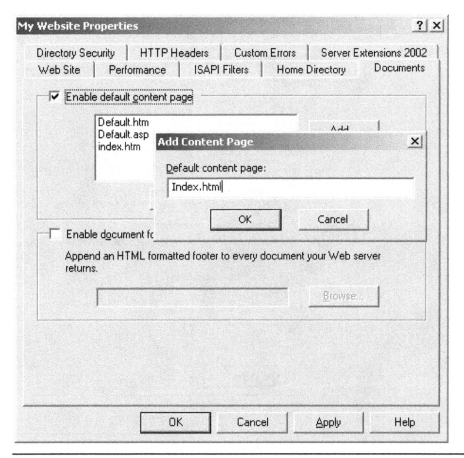

Figure 5.14: Adding a Context Page

The last major change to review in the IIS 6.0 properties is under the **Directory Security** tab (Figure 5.15). The authenticated access options have changed. Additionally, it should be noted that Microsoft has added built-in support for .NET Passport authentication, but not for competing authentication standards.

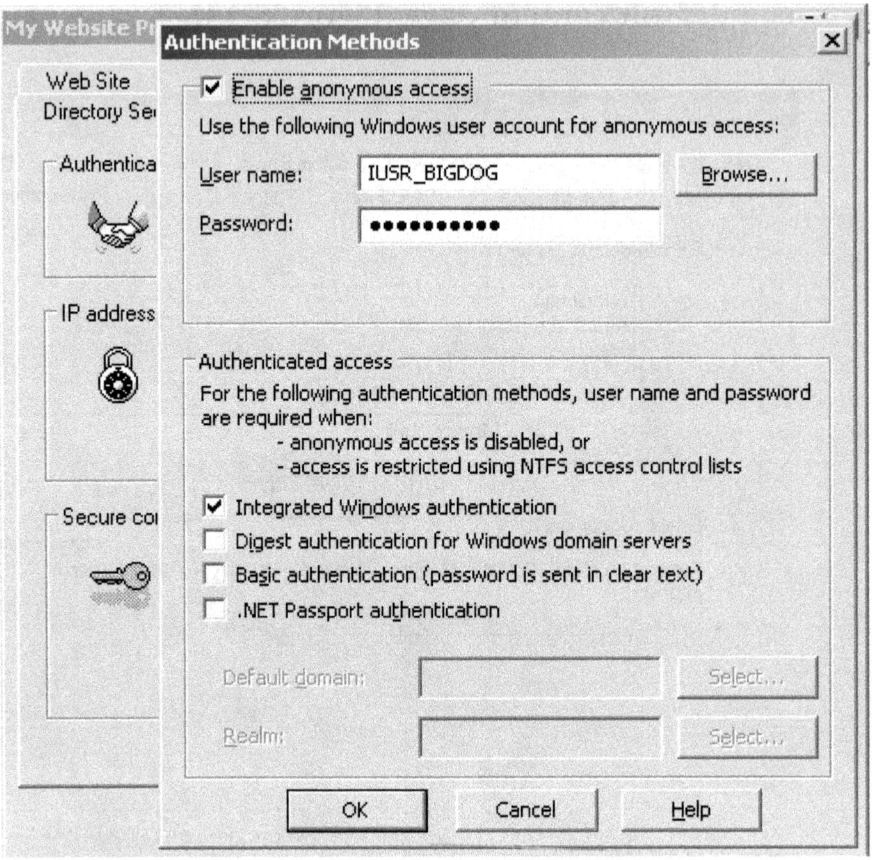

Figure 5.15: Directory Security - Authentication Methods

Summary

IIS 6.0 is installed in a more secure state than its predecessors. To provide a basic level of security, however, substantial reconfiguration is still recommended. The IIS Services Manager functions similar to the IIS 5.0 MMC snap-in. Through the IIS Services Manager both application pools and website are configured.

Chapter 6

Network Load Balancing

A recurring challenge with many of today's high volume websites is how to correct web servers that can no longer handle the amount of requests they receive. A system engineer typically has two options to address this very common problem. First, a newer and more powerful server can be installed to replace the overloaded-system. Alternately, an additional server can be added to load balance client requests.

Load Balancing Options

A load balancing technique called *Round Robin* is often used to manage requests between two or more web servers. Round Robin refers to the practice of using two or more IP addresses to resolve a single domain. For example, using Round Robin, the domain foo.com can resolve to both the IP addresses 10.80.1.100 and 10.80.1.101. Each time the DNS servers receives a request for foo.com, it alternates the IP address that is given to the requesting client machine. While this technique has been used to create web clusters successfully for many years, it does have several significant limitations.

Round Robin does not provide an effective load balancing solution because downstream DNS servers often cache DNS entries. When a DNS server caches an IP address, only the one IP address will be given out to all of the DNS server's client machines. This DNS caching results in an uneven distribution of client requests between servers.

Content Management

A more complicated issue for website management is keeping the content on both web servers identical. On NT-based systems a utility called *Robocopy* is an often-used tool for keeping web content synchronized. In enterprise networks a dedicated staging server is often set up where developers can publish new content. This staging server then copies data to all the web servers in the cluster, ensuring that the data remain synchronized on each server.

Managing Availability

Another major challenge web servers face is maintaining availability. Websites are a company's face to the public. If a potential customer goes to a company's website only to find that it is down, what does this say about the company's ability to run its business? Because of the potential to give customers a negative first impression, most companies demand near-perfect uptime for their web sites. Round Robin provides no failover; if one web server crashes the DNS server still gives out its IP address, resulting in half the users being directed to the non-responsive server.

The most common method of providing failover is to have two servers mirroring the same content in a load-balanced cluster. Both servers have private network connections allowing them to be updated from a staging server. Only the primary server has an active public connection to the Internet. In the event that the primary server crashes, an administrator assigns the secondary server's public interface the same IP address that the public interface on the primary server had, after which that interface is activated. This directs all the Internet traffic to the secondary server.

This type of failover is often accomplished by the use of home-grown scripts. The main drawback to this type of failover is that, even when using scripting, it takes several minutes to reconfigure the secondary server before service is restored. Following that, it takes several minutes of downtime while the primary server is brought back online. Also, if both the primary and secondary server's Internet-facing interface are inadvertently enabled at the same time, an IP conflict will occur and both servers will stop responding to requests, making the website unreachable. If an organization wants to provide both failover and load balancing for several websites, the resulting hodgepodge of configurations can become extremely difficult to manage. There is a definite need for a tool to automate cluster failover and load balancing.

Microsoft's Network Load Balancing Service

Microsoft has developed a simple service to address the common problems of load balancing and failover, the Network Load Balancing Service (NLBS). NLBS not only provides rudimentary load balancing, but also dynamic failover. NLBS allows organizations to cluster up to 32 Windows servers. NLBS enables administrators to add capacity to their web cluster by simply adding a new server configured with NLBS to the existing cluster. If a member of an NLBS cluster fails, NLBS automatically removes that server from the active web cluster until the server's operation is restored. While this book will focus on utilizing NLBS to work with web services, NLBS can easily be used for providing high availability and scalability to most TCP/IP-based services such as FTP servers, SMTP servers, even file and print servers.

NLBS is built into Microsoft's core operating system; it therefore requires no additional components to be purchased. NLBS can be used on Windows NT 4.0 server (on NT 4.0 it is called Windows Load Balancing Service), 2000 Advanced Server, or 2003 Enterprise and Data Center servers. It is installed as a network service under the Network Connections Property window box.

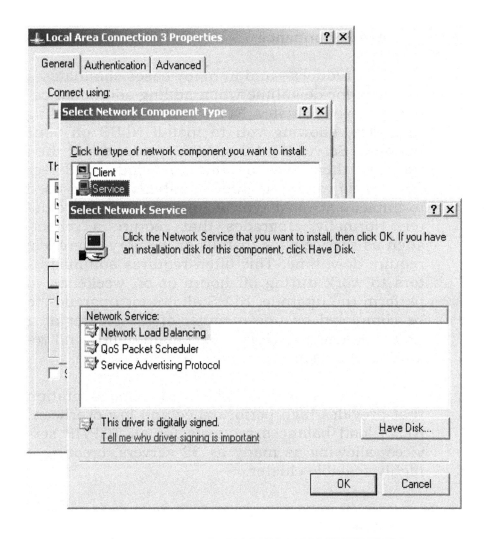

Figure 6.1: Installing Network Load Balancing on Windows 2000

The major benefits of NLBS Include:

■ Scalable performance

■ High availability

■ Highly configurable

Scalable Performance

NLBS reduces—and in many cases eliminates—the need for downtime when adding additional capacity to your cluster. NLBS even allows for rolling upgrades, allowing you to install NLBS on your Windows Server NT 4.0 or 2000 systems and then upgrade them one by one to Windows Server 2003. This rolling upgrade capability can be used to implement most typical upgrades to your cluster. Normally, upgrades that require a reboot, such as service pack installs or memory upgrades, require downtime. This often requires administrators to work during off hours or on weekends to perform the upgrade. NLBS allows for upgrades to be completed on one member of the cluster at a time, allowing the cluster to remain online and resulting in zero downtime during the upgrade.

NLBS uses a fully pipelined implementation that provides high performance and low overhead. NLBS load balances requests for all TCP/IP services, allowing as many as 32 servers, creating a highly scalable cluster.

High Availability

In an NLBS cluster any server that fails or goes offline will automatically be removed from the cluster. Furthermore, once the server comes back online NLBS will automatically start directing requests to the server again, without administrator intervention. When a new server is added to the cluster NLBS automatically re-distributes client requests on the fly. NLBS is even able to handle multiple simultaneous outages and inadvertent network changes.

Highly Configurable

NLBS allows for easy configuration of both TCP and UDP ports. NLBS allows for load weighting, where each server is assigned a numerical value to determine the percentage of the HTTP requests it receives. This feature is useful for balancing the load across several servers with different configurations. For example, it allows an Itanium server to be added to an existing cluster, giving it a high load weight that allows the Itanium server to receive a higher percentage of the client requests. Similarly, older low-end servers can be given a low load weight and be primarily used in case of a spike in the number of visitors to a website.

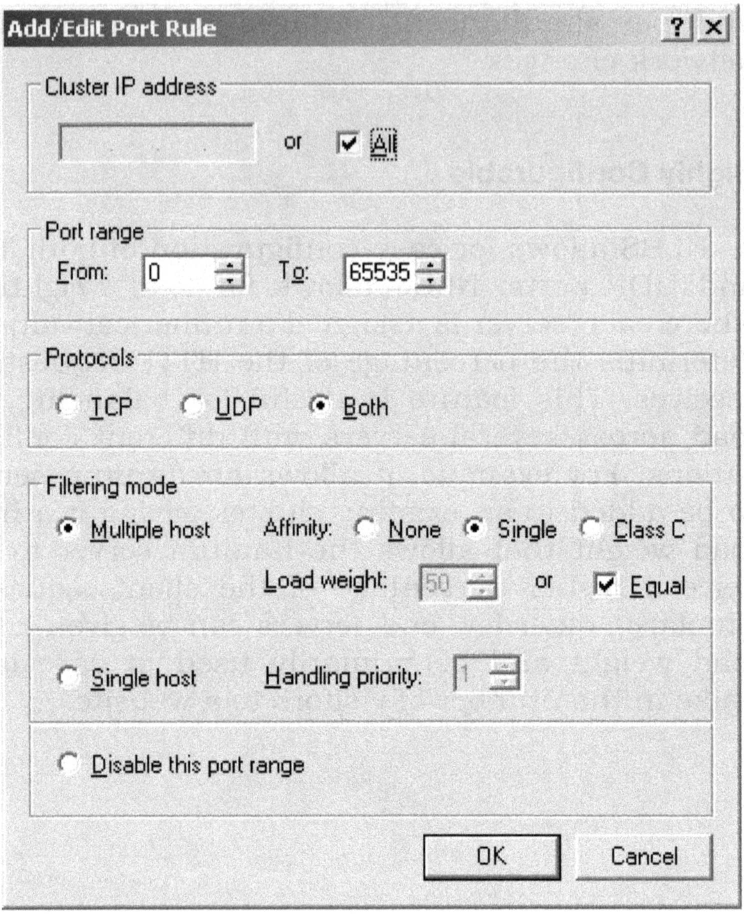

Figure 6.2: Windows 2000 Network Load Balancing Service Configuration

NLBS supports Secure Socket Layer (SSL) and client affinity. Enabling client affinity allows users to maintain session state; once a user is directed by NLBS to a given server, all future requests are forwarded to the same server. Session state is required for using advanced features such as ASPs. Websites often use these programs for shopping carts, message boards, and to provide personalized content. If client affinity is not required for a website to function properly, it is recommended that it not be used, because disabling client affinity allows for improved load balancing.

Hardware Load Balancing

Products such as Cisco's Local Director and Big IP's f5 offer hardware load balancing solutions. The main advantage to these hardware-based solutions is that they have zero server overhead. Hardware-based load balancing solutions also work farther up the network stack. While these solutions work effectively, they are also cost prohibitive. Given, the low overhead and robustness of Microsoft's NLBS, the cost effectiveness of hardware load balancing appliances should be closely scrutinized before a purchase decision is made.

Unix Load Balancing

Since NT-based systems often have to share space on the data center floor, a brief discussion regarding Unix load balancing is required. Under Unix, load balancing is most often accomplished using either Round Robin, or a hardware-based solution, such as the solutions discussed in the previous paragraph. The main drawback with Round Robin is that it provides no failover protection. If even one member of a cluster fails, some users will still be directed to the non-functional server.

Several software solutions are being developed to address this Unix deficiency. The leading solution is an open-source project called *Backhand*. Backhand is available at no cost for Linux, Solaris, and several different implementations of

BSD, even NT. Backhand creates a cluster of web servers with a single shared IP address, similar to Microsoft's NLBS. Backhand automatically load balances HTTP requests according to server resource availability. Backhand examines each cluster member's available memory, processing power, and Input/Output to determine which server receives any given request. Backhand is also highly configurable, allowing an administrator to customize its operation. Backhand's major drawback is that, due to its complexity, it takes a knowledgeable administrator to install and properly configure the application.

All the Backhand executables and source code can be downloaded from www.backhand.org.

Leveraging High-End Servers in Network Load Balancing Clusters

Proper utilization of high-end servers in a network can result in substantial cost savings as well as an increase in system availability. Xeon or even Itanium servers can be used to replace older servers or to supplement an existing cluster. Because of the power of Itanium servers, it may be advantageous to completely re-design a network to take full advantage of this scalability.

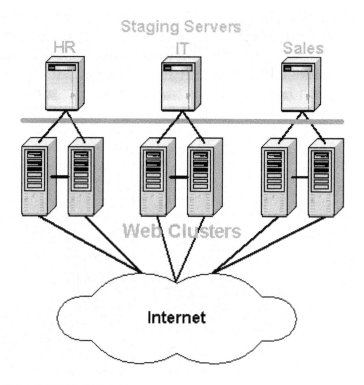

Figure 6.3: Conventional Cluster Scenario

Typically, each department's website is housed in its own cluster, as seen in Figure 6.3. By replacing the existing web servers with powerful high-end servers, one cluster now has the power to host several different websites. Additionally, because of the decrease in the number of separate clusters the number of staging servers can also be reduced. In the example in Figure 6.4 the number of servers needed to maintain redundancy and load balancing has been reduced by 66%.

The benefit of using high-end servers is dependant on the complexity of the website. A complex website utilizing numerous COM objects or

Secure Sockets Layer (SSL) might benefit from an XEON or Itanium-based solution. On the other hand, a simple site serving static HTML pages would most likely see little or no benefit from the increased horsepower that a new server provides.

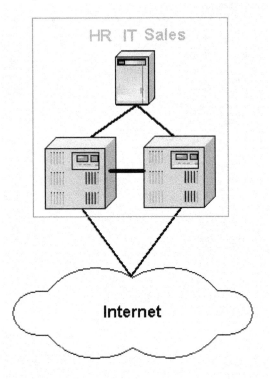

Figure 6.4: Consolidated Web Cluster

Network Load Balancing Service Scenarios

Multi-homed Websites with NLBS

When configuring multi-homed websites with NLBS, setting client affinity to **None**, unless it is required, is generally preferred. Each additional website's IP address should be set up under the

Advanced tab of the **TCP/IP Properties** dialog box and IIS should be configured as it would be for a stand-alone, multi-homed web server. No additional special configuration is required for most multi-homed clusters.

Active Server Pages (ASP)

Active Server Pages usually require client affinity; most often affinity should be set to **Single**, or **Class C**. It is possible that users who are behind multiple proxy servers may have their connections appear to be coming from multiple IP addresses. There are several solutions to this problem. Usually setting client affinity to Class C will resolve this issue. However, the Class C setting limits the ability of NLBS to load balance clients evenly. Another solution is to use programming to enable the client to maintain client affinity through the use of a cookie or client-side solution.

Streaming media

NLBS is well suited for serving streaming media. Administrators should be aware that when adding servers to a streaming media cluster that is serving media using the UDP protocol, active clients stream might be interrupted. To avoid client interruptions, adding servers to streaming media clusters only when no clients are connected, or during low traffic periods, is recommended.

Virtual Private Networks and Secure Socket Layer

Virtual Private Networks (VPN) and Secure Socket Layer (SSL), both require client affinity to be set to **Single**. For SSL the port range should be set to 443, for VPN set the port range to that used by your VPN application. If the VPN port is unknown or is variable, the port can be set to the default, 0-65535. If a member of a cluster fails while handling a secure connection, users will automatically be redirected to another server in the cluster and required to login again in order to restart their session.

Other Applications

Although not common, other TCP and UDP applications can be used with NLBS. One example is file servers that serve archived information to a large number of users, provided that they connect using a DNS name. Flat databases such as those used with XML can use NLBS as long as they are read-only. Applications such as SMTP are also ideal candidates to use NLBS.

Summary

Network load balancing and Internet Information Server version 6.0 are a powerful combination, enabling an organization to save money while increasing redundancy and simplifying scalability. Microsoft's NLBS allows up to 32 servers to be clustered together, taking scalability to a new level. NLBS allows for the flexibility and backward compatibility that is needed in today's rapidly changing web architecture.

Chapter 7

Network Load Balancing Configuration

Windows Server 2000 requires Network Load Balancing to be added on after the initial OS build was completed, installed from the **Network Properties** dialog box. In Windows Server 2003 Network Load Balancing is installed by default and managed via the **Network Load Balancing (NLB) Manager**. The NLB Manager may appear confusing at first glance once mastered; it simplifies the management of NLB clusters by offering a GUI interface as well as a wizard to assist with configuring new clusters.

Getting Started

The NLB Manager can be started from the **Start** menu by selecting; **Start**, **Administrative Tools**, **Network Load Balancing Manager**. The NLBS Manager displays the name of each cluster, basic configuration data as well as error and status messages.

New Cluster Wizard

Once in the NLB Manager the **New Cluster Wizard** can be started by right-clicking **Network Load Balancing Clusters** in the left pane and selecting **New Cluster**, as shown in Figure 7.1.

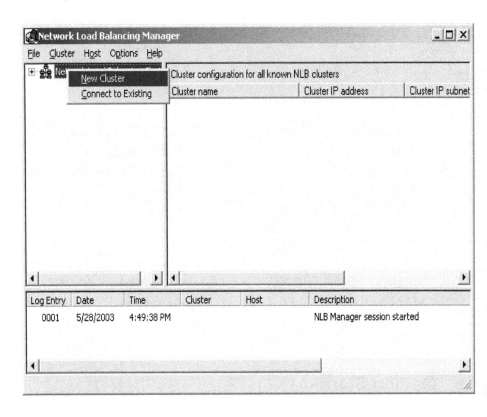

Figure 7.1: Network Load Balancing Manager

The **Cluster Parameters** window will be presented as the first window of the New Cluster Wizard (Figure 7.2). The **Cluster IP configuration** section is where **IP address** information for the shared cluster IP address, the virtual IP, is entered. Do not enter the local machine's IP address in this window. For this example, use 192.168.1.10 with a **Subnet mask** of 255.255.255.0. The **Full Internet name** is the DNS name of the cluster, in this example use foo.com.

Cluster operation mode should normally be left to **Unicast**. **Multicast** and IGMP multicast are specialized technologies used for sending one data stream to multiple clients over a TCP/IP network. Many routers in use today do not support multicast and its implementation is beyond the scope of this book

Due to security concerns, enabling the **Allow remote control** option is not recommended on most networks. On networks without physical network isolation, Microsoft cautions against using this option. Disabling this option will prevent users from remotely managing the cluster using NLB.exe, which is discussed in the next section, *Command-Line Management.*

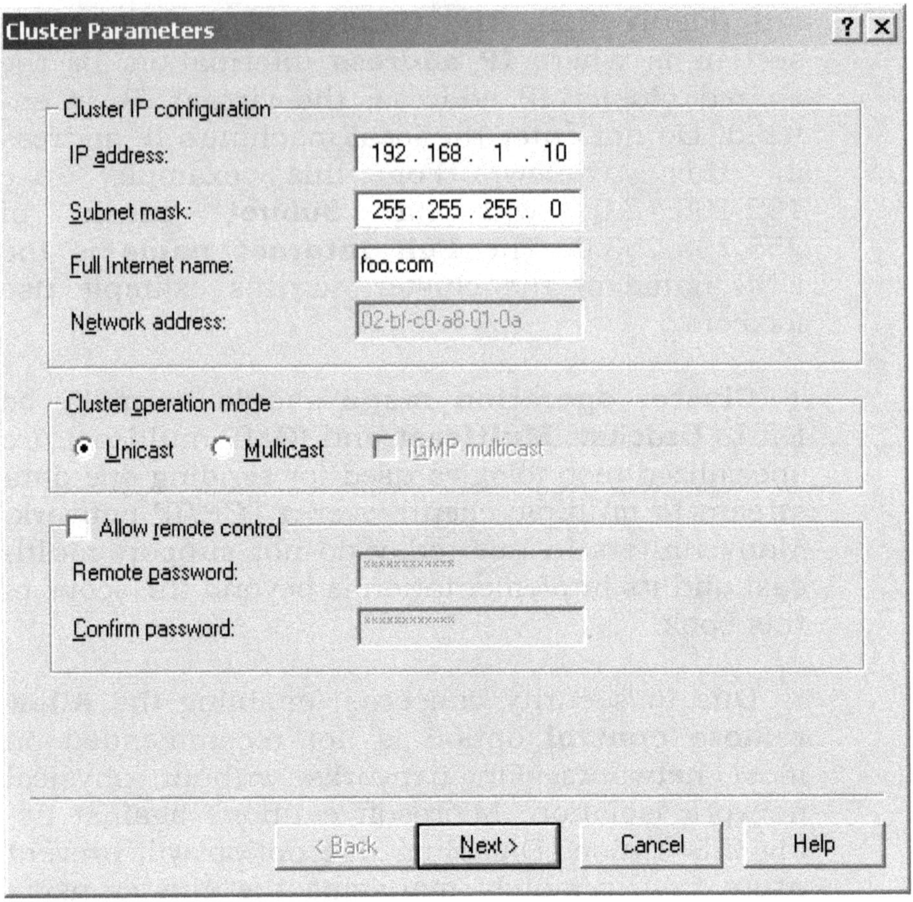

Figure 7.2: Cluster Parameters

The next screen, **Cluster IP Addresses**, will prompt for the addition of additional virtual IP addresses. This allows for one cluster to provide NLB service for multiple virtual IP addresses. Typical NLB installations do not use additional IP addresses. Click **Next** without adding addition IP information in this window (Figure 7.3).

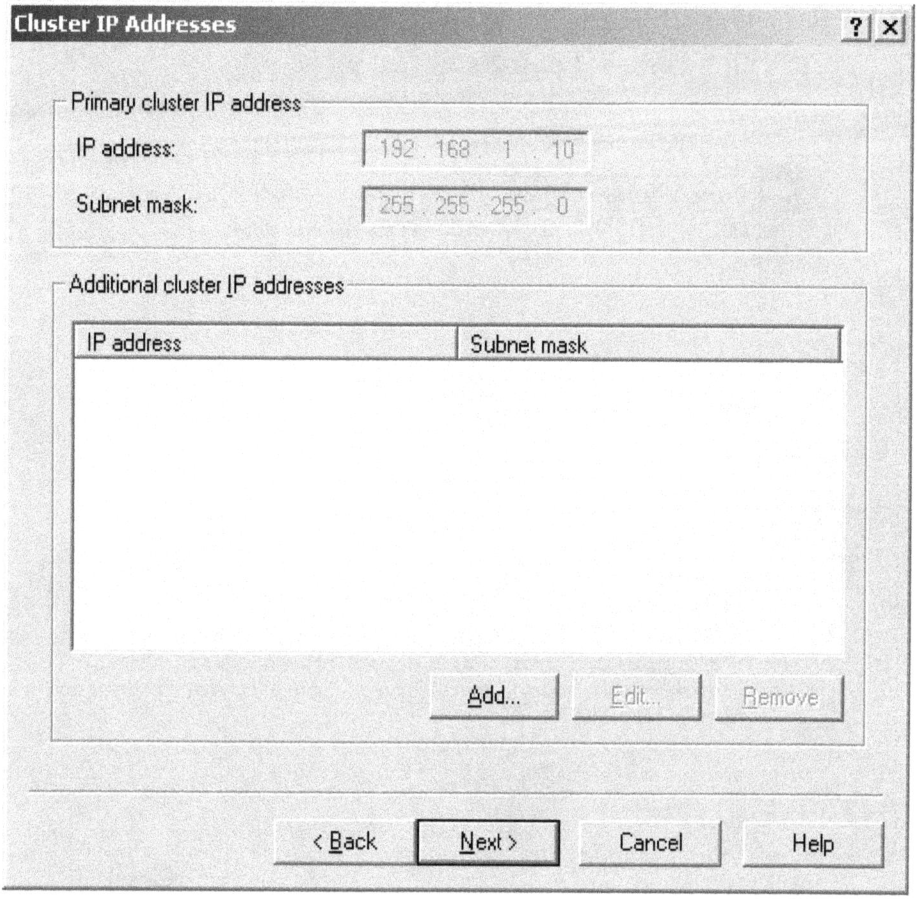

Cluster IP Addresses ? X

Primary cluster IP address

IP address: 192 . 168 . 1 . 10

Subnet mask: 255 . 255 . 255 . 0

Additional cluster IP addresses

IP address	Subnet mask

Add... Edit... Remove

< Back | Next > | Cancel | Help

Figure 7.3: Cluster IP Addresses

The **Port Rules** window is displayed in Figure 7.4. By default, all ports, both TCP and UDP, are routed though the cluster. Clicking **Edit** allows the port rules to be modified. For example, a company may want to only load balance TCP traffic designated for port 80 in a cluster. To accomplish this, the port range would have to be changed to: From 80, To 80 and under **Protocols**, **TCP** would be selected, as shown in Figure 7.5.

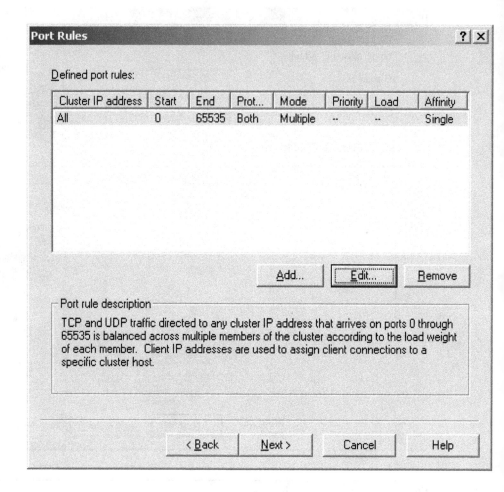

Figure 7.4: Port Rules Window

From this window client affinity can also be configured under **Filtering Mode**. Client affinity insures that multiple requests from a single client are all routed to the same NLBS Member. Client affinity is covered in Chapter 6 *Network Load Balancing*. For this example set the client **Affinity** to **Single**.

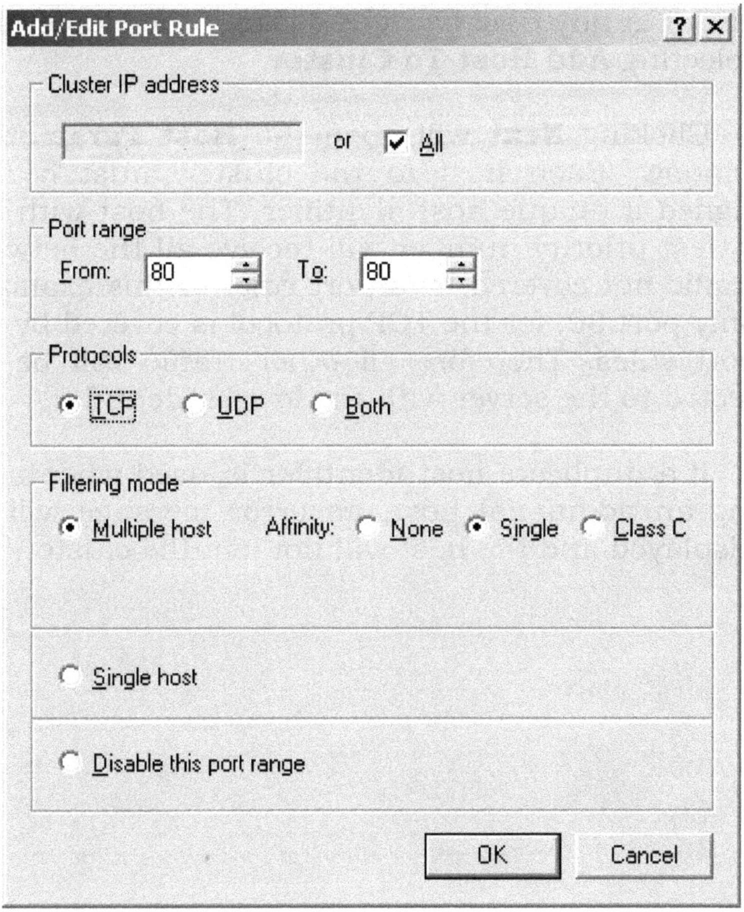

Figure 7.5: Add or Edit Port Rules

The **Connect** window allows the IP address information for each member of the cluster to be entered. Hosts can only be added by entering the Host name or Host IP address. Enter the name of the first member of the cluster and click **Connect**. From the dropdown list select the interface that is to be used with the cluster. Remember, all cluster interfaces must be configured with static IP addresses. Additional members of the cluster can be added at any time by right-clicking the cluster and selecting **Add Host To Cluster**.

Clicking **Next** will open the **Host Parameters** window. Each host in the cluster must be assigned a unique host identifier. The host with the lowest priority number will receive all the network traffic not covered by a port rule. In this example, only port 80, for the TCP protocol is covered by the port rules. Therefore all other traffic will be directed to the server with the lowest identifier.

If a duplicate host identifier is used when adding an additional host, an error message will be displayed and the host will not join the cluster.

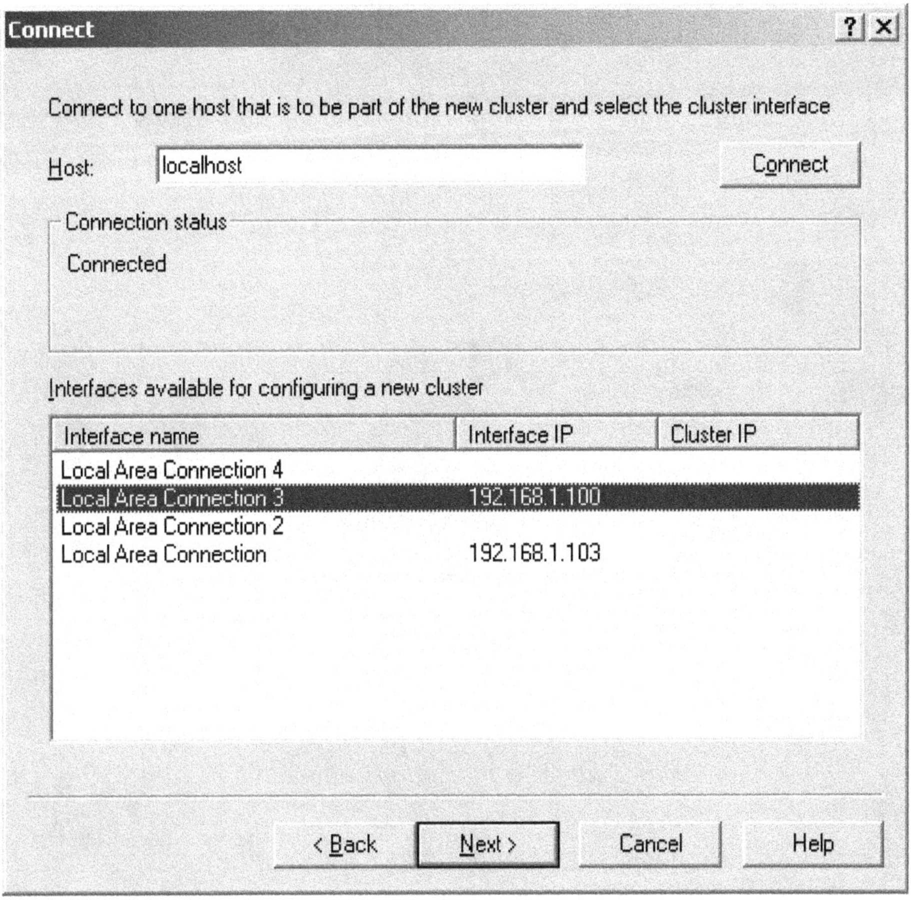

Figure 7.6: Connect to Local Host

The **Initial host state** determines the state that the host will be in once the wizard closes. Normally, this should be left to **Started**, unless the cluster will not be enabled until a later date, in which event the host state should be set to **Stop** or **Suspended**.

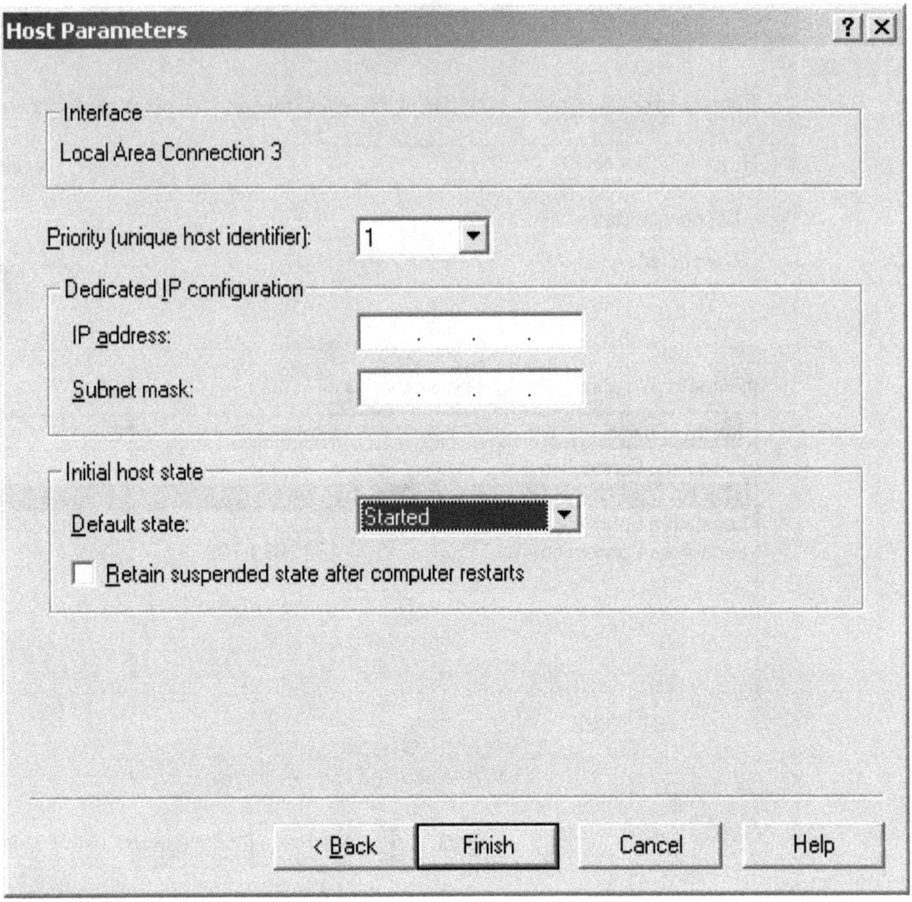

Host Parameters   **?** **X**

Interface

Local Area Connection 3

Priority (unique host identifier):   `1` ▼

Dedicated IP configuration

IP address: `.    .    .`

Subnet mask: `.    .    .`

Initial host state

Default state: `Started` ▼

☐ Retain suspended state after computer restarts

     < Back   Finish   Cancel   Help

Figure 7.7: Host Parameters

Clicking the **Finish** button will close the New Cluster Wizard. The new cluster will automatically register and initialize the cluster. This process may take several minutes. Any error messages will appear in the bottom pane of the NLBS manager window. Double-clicking on any message that appears in this bottom pane will open a new window with detailed information on the message.

Note that these messages do not automatically update at regular intervals. The NLBS manager must be manually updated by selecting **Cluster**, **Refresh** from the toolbar. Unlike other Microsoft applications, pressing the F5 key will not automatically refresh the screen.

New members of the cluster can be added at any time by selecting the cluster name from the left pane, right-clicking the name and then selecting, **Add Host To Cluster**. This will open the new cluster **Connect** window seen in Figure 7.6. Additionally, the next time the NLBS Manager is restarted the existing cluster(s) will have to be reregistered by right-clicking on **Network Load Balancing Cluster** and selecting **Connect to Existing**. The user can then enter the cluster's host name and reconnect to the cluster.

Command-Line Management

In Windows Server 2003 Microsoft includes a command-line utility called NLB.exe for managing NLBS. NLB.exe simplifies the task of performing routine maintenance tasks. For security reasons NLB.exe should usually not be configured to allow remote management of NLB clusters.

NLB.exe can be used to perform most cluster management tasks, such as enabling or disabling the cluster, reconfiguring port-handling configurations, or querying the status of the cluster. The next section displays the output of the NLB.exe help file:

WLBS Cluster Control Utility V2.4 (c) 1997-2003 Microsoft Corporation.
Usage: WLBS <command> [/PASSW [<password>]] [/PORT <port>]

```
<command>
  help                          - displays this help
  ip2mac   <cluster>              - displays the MAC address for the
                                specified cluster
  reload   [<cluster> | ALL]      - reloads the driver's parameters from
                                the registry for the specified
                                cluster (local only). Same as ALL if
                                parameter is not specified.
  display  [<cluster> | ALL]      - displays configuration parameters,
                                current status, and last several
                                event log messages for the specified
                                cluster (local only). Same as ALL if
                                parameter is not specified.
  query    [<cluster_spec>]       - displays the current cluster state
                                for the current members of the
                                specified cluster. If not specified a
                                local query is performed for all
                                instances.
  suspend  [<cluster_spec>]       - suspends cluster operations (start,
                                stop, etc.) for the specified cluster
                                until the resume command is issued.
                                If cluster is not specified, applies
                                to all instances on local host.
  resume   [<cluster_spec>]       - resumes cluster operations after a
                                previous suspend command for the
                                specified cluster. If cluster is not
                                specified, applies to all instances
                                on local host.
  start    [<cluster_spec>]       - starts cluster operations on the
                                specified hosts. Applies to local
                                host if cluster is not specified.
  stop     [<cluster_spec>]       - stops cluster operations on the
                                specified hosts. Applies to local
```

host if cluster is not specified.

drainstop [<cluster_spec>]   - disables all new traffic handling on
                                          the specified hosts and stops cluster
                                          operations. Applies to local host if
                                          cluster is not specified.

enable   <port_spec> <cluster_spec> - enables traffic handling on the
                                          specified cluster for the rule whose
                                          port range contains the specified
                                          port

disable   <port_spec> <cluster_spec>   - disables ALL traffic handling on
   the
                                          specified cluster for the rule whose
                                          port range contains the specified
                                          port

drain   <port_spec> <cluster_spec>   - disables NEW traffic handling on
   the
                                          specified cluster for the rule whose
                                          port range contains the specified
                                          port

queryport [<vip>:]<port>   - retrieve the current state of the
         [<cluster_spec>]   port rule. If the rule is handling
                                          traffic, packet handling statistics
                                          are also returned.

params [<cluster> | ALL]   - retrieve the current parameters from
                                          the NLB driver for the specified
                                          cluster on the local host.

<port_spec>
 [<vip>: | ALL:](<port> | ALL)   - every virtual ip address (neither
                                          <vip> nor ALL) or specific <vip> or
                                          the "All" vip, on a specific <port>
                                          rule or ALL ports

<cluster_spec>
 <cluster>:<host> | ((<cluster> | ALL) - specific <cluster> on a specific
 (LOCAL | GLOBAL))   <host>, OR specific <cluster> or ALL

clusters, on the LOCAL machine or all (GLOBAL) machines that are a part of the cluster

<cluster>   - cluster name | cluster primary IP address

<host>   - host within the cluster (default - ALL hosts): dedicated name | IP address | host priority ID (1..32) | 0 for current DEFAULT host

<vip>   - virtual ip address in the port rule

<port>   - TCP/UDP port number

Remote options:

/PASSW <password>   - remote control password (default - NONE)

blank <password> for console prompt

/PORT <port>   - cluster's remote control UDP port

For detailed information, see the online help for NLB.

Information on cluster error messages, cluster operation and additional options can be found in Microsoft's Cluster help files, conveniently accessed via the NLB Manager by selecting **Help**, **Help Topics**. The help file includes a section to assist users experienced with NLBS on Windows Server 2000, titled: *New ways to do familiar tasks.*

Summary

The NLB Manager simplifies the tasks of setting up and configuring network load balancing clusters. Users familiar with NLBS on Windows Server 4.0 or 2000 may find the help section, *New ways to do familiar tasks*, helpful in transitioning to this new tool. The command-line management tool NLB.exe simplifies cluster management. It does not, however, allow for secure remote cluster management.

Chapter 8

Simple Mail Transport Protocol (SMTP) Service

IIS 6.0 includes a built-in Simple Mail Transfer Protocol (SMTP) service for routing and delivery of e-mail messages. Microsoft's SMTP service is designed primarily for forwarding outgoing mail. Although Microsoft's SMTP service is not designed to handle incoming user mail, it will accept any incoming mail addressed to its default domain. This mail, however, will be routed to a generic Drop folder, not to an individual user. Individual mailboxes can be set up to handle multiple users' e-mail using either Microsoft Exchange Server, or Microsoft's new POP3 service for Windows Server 2003.

SMTP Overview

Microsoft's SMTP server is designed to be fully configurable, yet once set up requires little—if any—maintenance. When running, the service automatically monitors a designated folder for outgoing messages. When a message is placed in this directory, the SMTP service automatically resolves the domain name and forwards the mail directory to the appropriate domain, based on the recipient's e-mail address. The message header must be formatted correctly. A sample message header is displayed in the next section.

```
X-sender: postmaster@foo.com

X-receiver: mike@foo.com

From: postmaster@foo.com

To: mike@foo.com

Subject: Hi!


How are you doing today?
```

Default Folders

When configured, the SMTP service creates several subfolders under a user-specified root directory. These folders include the previous incoming and outgoing mail folders discussed in the previous section, as well as several other folders.

- Drop – Incoming e-mail folder. All e-mail addressed to the default domain is automatically delivered to this folder, regardless of username.

- Pickup – Any messages placed in this folder are automatically routed to the recipient. All outgoing mail should be placed it this folder.

- Badmail – All undeliverable e-mail is placed in this folder. This includes messages with bad headers, unknown recipients, and failed deliveries. Undeliverable messages can be identified by the extension .BAD. The corresponding error message can be found in the file with the same name, and a .BDR extension.

- Queue – All messages that are not immediately delivered are placed in the queue directory. Messages may be placed in this directory for a variety of reasons, including failed delivery attempts or Internet connection outage. The SMTP service will automatically attempt to resend these messages, depending on the SMTP site configuration.

- Mailbox, Route & SortTemp – These directories are no longer used by the current version of SMTP and messages will not normally be placed in these directories.

SMTP Virtual Server Wizard

To create a new virtual SMTP server, right-click the default SMTP icon and select **New**, **Virtual Server**, as shown in Figure 8.1. This will open the **New SMTP Virtual Server Wizard** (Figure 8.2). The name of the virtual server should be concise but descriptive. In this example the domain name mail.foo.com will be used. Note that for the domain name mail.foo.com to function properly, it must be a valid domain name.

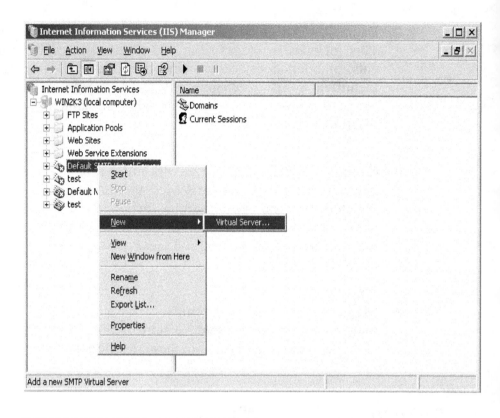

Figure 8.1: Internet Information Services (IIS) Manager

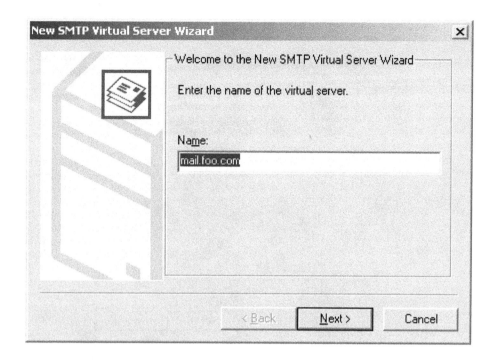

Figure 8.2: New SMTP Virtual Server Wizard

After entering the domain name, click **Next**. If the server has more than one IP address assigned to its NIC or more than one NIC installed, select the correct IP address for this SMTP server here. Machines with a single IP address may chose to leave the default (**All Unassigned**).

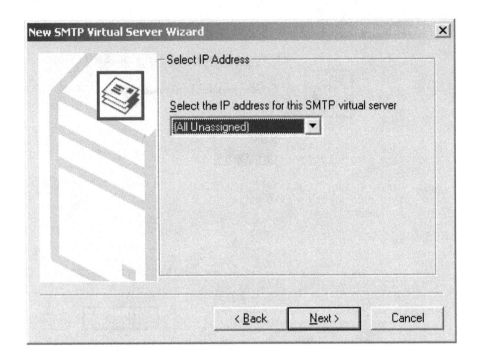

Figure 8.3: Select IP address

If another Virtual SMTP site exists on the same IP address, the warning message shown in Figure 8.4 will be displayed. This is because in Chapter 6 the default virtual SMTP site was disabled. The default virtual SMTP site cannot be deleted, but if disabled will not conflict with the mail.foo.com virtual SMTP site. Therefore, click **Yes** to bypass this message.

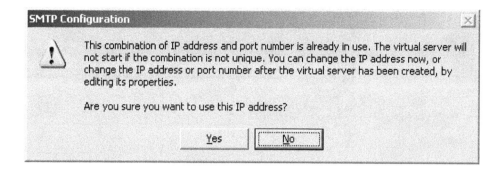

Figure 8.4: SMTP Configuration Warning

The **Select Home Directory** window, shown in Figure 8.5 is used to specify the directory where the SMTP root folder will be located. Any user who wishes to access SMTP services on this server will need to have access to this folder and its subdirectories. Therefore, this folder should be located in a convenient location with proper permissions. The directory must already exist; it cannot be created through the New Virtual SMTP Site Wizard.

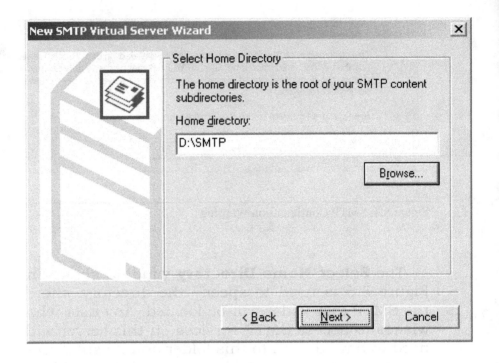

Figure 8.5 Select Home Directory

Clicking **Next** will bring up the default domain for this virtual SMTP server. This should be the primary domain for which this virtual server will be handling mail transfers. Often, this is simply the root domain; in this example, foo.com.

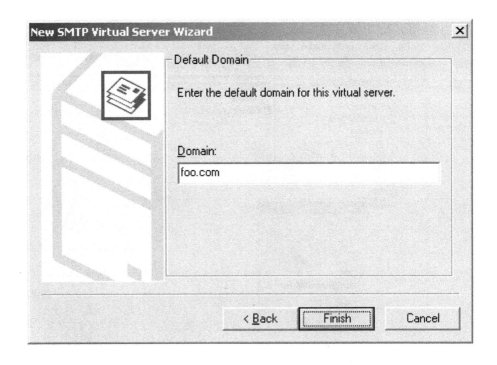

Figure 8.6: Default Domain

Clicking **Finish** will create the mail.foo.com virtual SMTP site. Because the default virtual server is set to **Disabled**, this virtual SMTP server will also initially be disabled. Right-clicking the name or icon for a virtual server will allow it to be enabled.

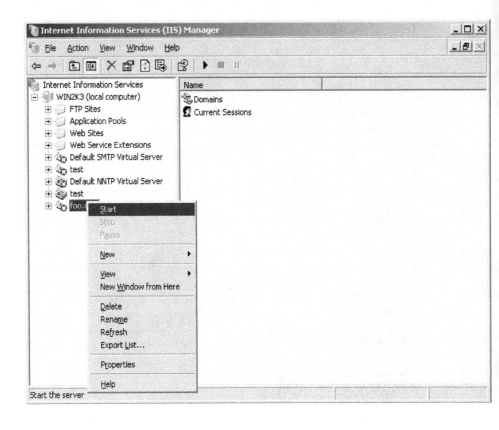

Figure 8.7: Opening the SMTP Properties Window

Configuring a Virtual SMTP Server

Right-clicking a mail site (as shown in Figure 8.7) and clicking **Properties** will bring up the **Properties** window for any given domain. The SMTP properties are divided into six tabs; **General**, **Access**, **Messages**, **Delivery**, **LDAP Routing** and **Security**.

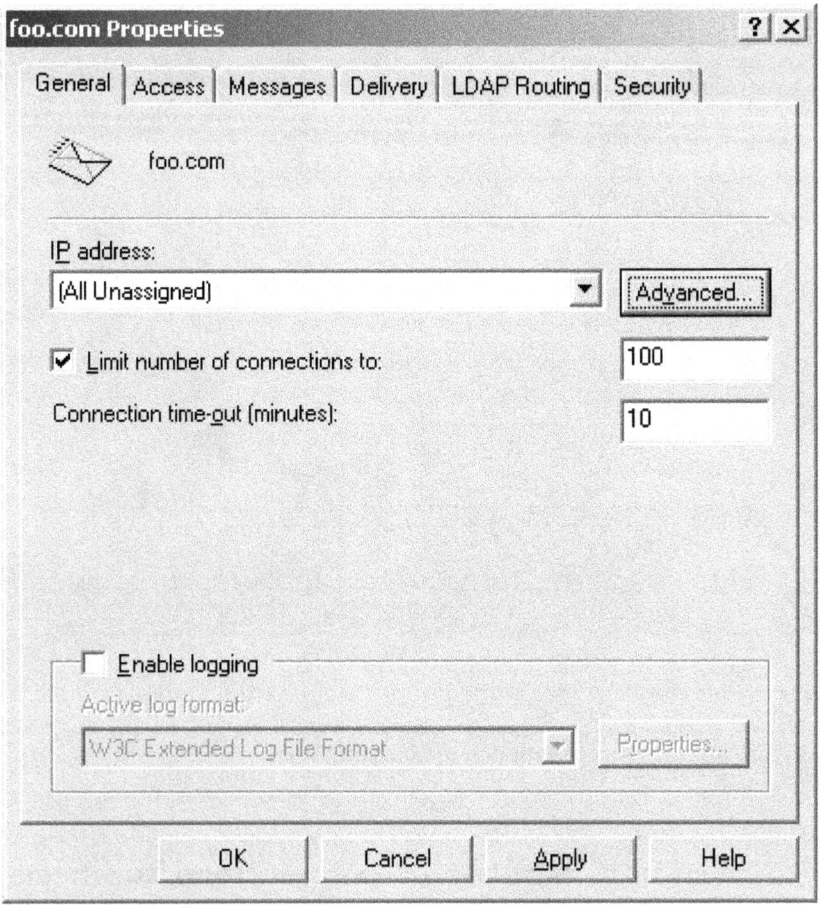

Figure 8.8: General Tab

General

The **General** tab allows the SMTP server's IP address to be configured. By clicking **Advanced** the SMTP port can be changed. The default port for all SMTP servers is 25 and normally will not be changed.

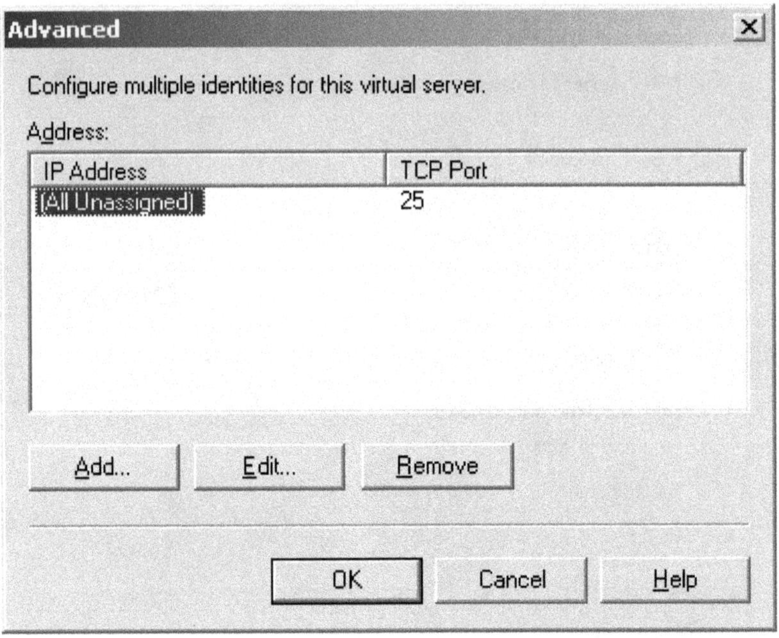

Figure 8.9: Advanced Option in the General Tab

The **Limit number of connections to** check-box allows an administrator to limit the number of connections to the SMTP server. Unless the server is to be used as a dedicated SMTP server, it is recommended that a limit is placed on the number of connections. The last option, **Enable Logging,** enables logging. Several different log formats are available.

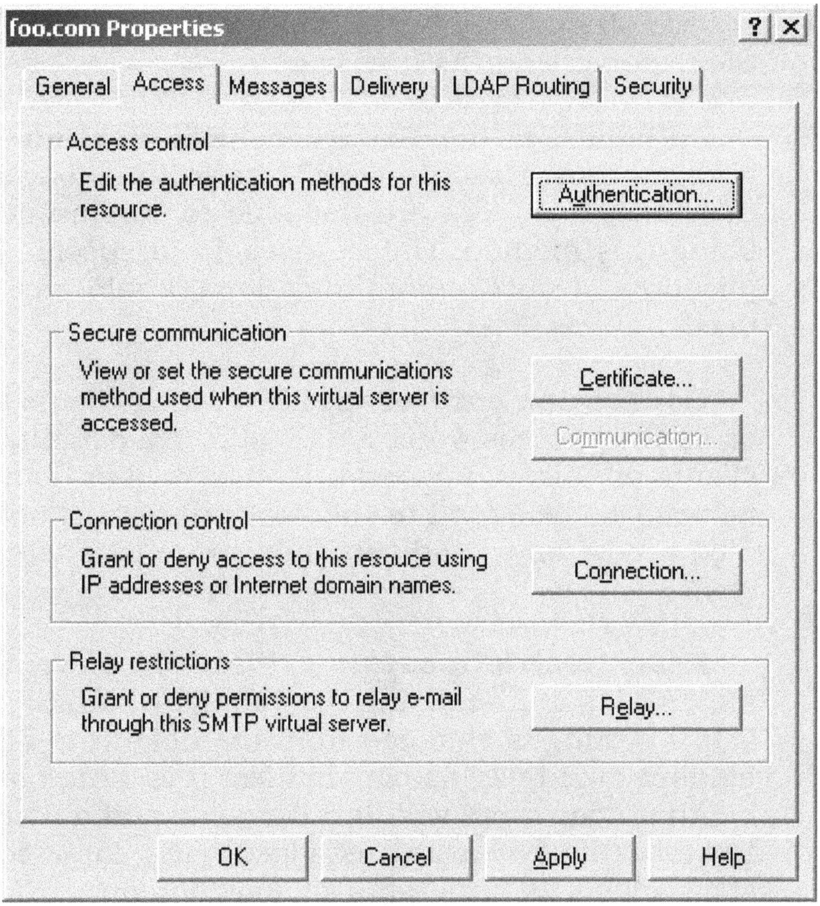

Figure 8.10: Access Tab

Access

The **Access** tab allows the configuration of different access and communication parameters. The **Access control** section allows the authentication method to be defined. This selection should normally be left on the default, **Anonymous** access. Requiring authentication will prevent the SMTP service from communicating with most other SMTP servers on the Internet.

Additionally, the **Secure communication** option requires a secure certificate to function, and most SMTP servers are not able to communicate using this method. Unless used for a specific application, secure communication should not be used.

Connection control specifies which clients can or cannot access your SMTP site. By default, all clients are allowed access. IP addresses or domain names can be added to the list and granted or denied access on an individual or group (subnet) basis.

Relay restrictions are critical for preventing the SMTP site from being used to distribute SPAM. If this setting is changed from the default to allow blanket mail relaying capabilities, it is quite possible that spammers will find the relay and abuse it. Unscrupulous users engaged in large-scale spamming run programs to look for open SMTP relays. Because of the potential for misuse, leave the relay restrictions in place for all servers connected to the Internet.

Messages

The **Messages** tab configures parameters for inbound and outbound mail. For most SMTP servers the defaults will function correctly. However, for some custom applications it may be prudent to change these settings.

Limit message size to specifies the maximum size of e-mail messages. Any message exceeding this value will automatically be rejected. If large files such as uncompressed log files are regularly transferred, this setting might need to be raised.

Limit Session Size specifies the size limit for all messages transferred during a single session. For example, if six 2MB messages are attempted to be sent on a SMTP site with a 10MB limit, the connection will be closed once the limit is reached and the last message will not be sent.

Limit number of messages per connection limits the number of e-mail messages that are set in one connection. This setting cannot be used to prevent a large number of messages being set at once. When the limit is reached the SMTP service will simply start a new connection and continue to process the remaining messages.

Limit the number of recipients per message to limits the number of users that can be sent a single e-mail using one connection. Like the previous setting, this setting cannot be used to limit the number of recipients. If this limit is reached the SMTP service will simply open a new connection and continue sending the e-mail message to the remaining recipients.

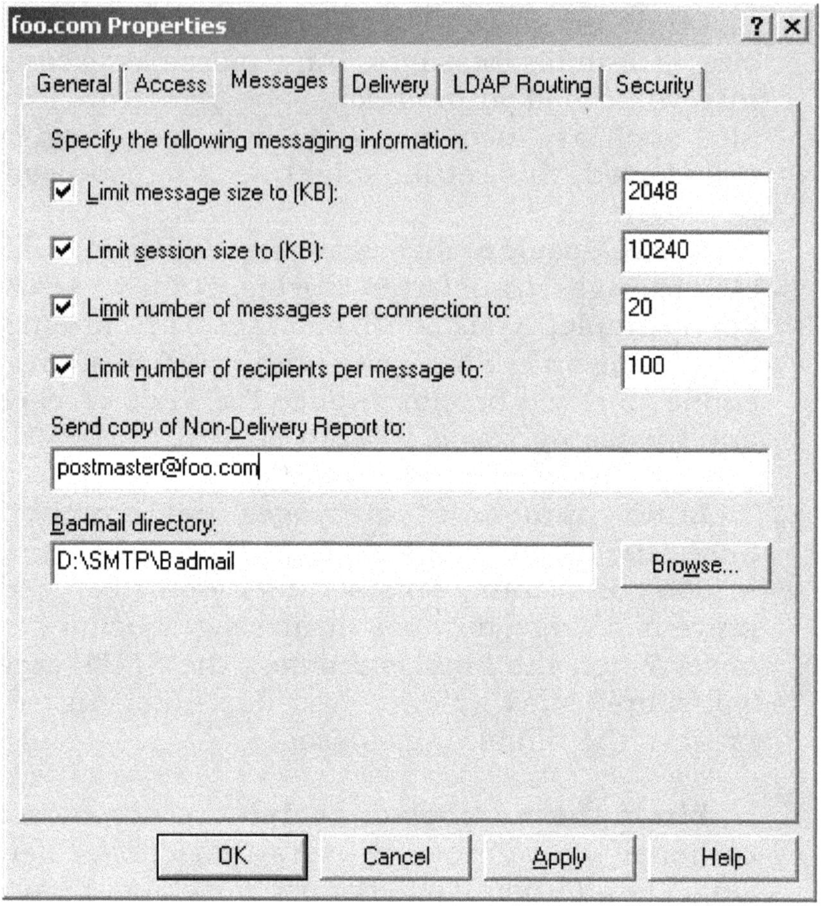

Figure 8.11: Messages Tab

The **Send Non-delivery Report to** field allows the administrator to specify the e-mail address of the postmaster, or system administrator. This e-mail address will be notified any time there is a message delivery failure. The folder that error messages are placed in can be relocated by changing the **Badmail directory** field.

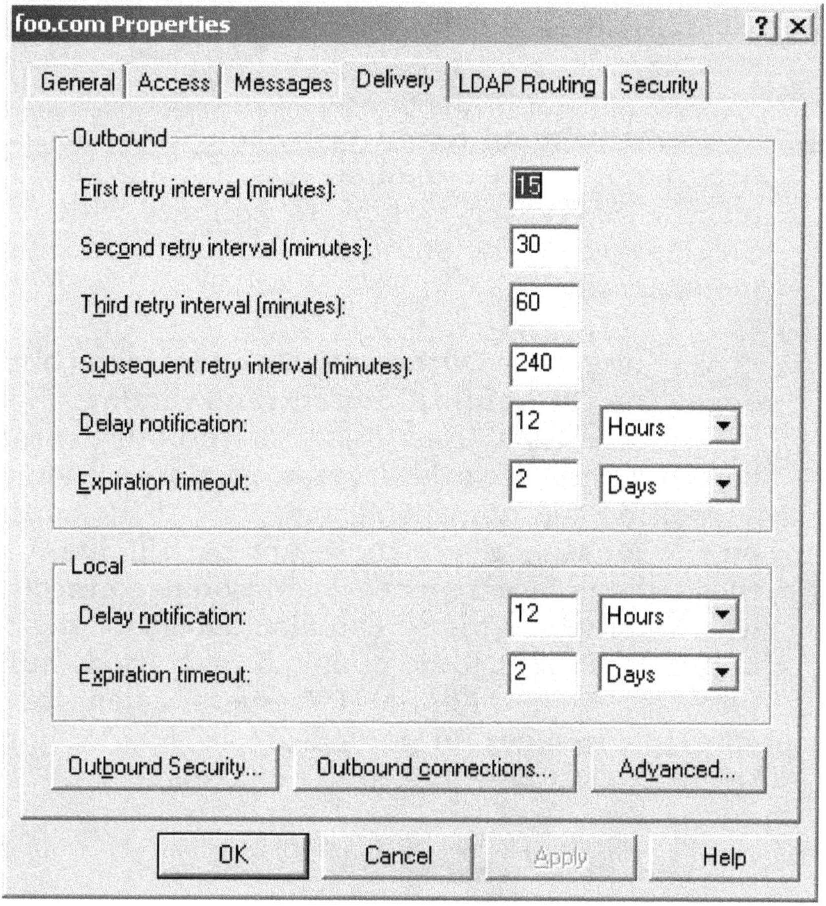

Figure 8.12: Delivery Tab

Delivery

The **Delivery** tab controls the various settings for e-mail delivery and routing. The first group of settings, labeled **Outbound,** configures the outgoing mail delivery attempt options. The default settings are appropriate for most SMTP implementations. The second set of settings, **Local**, configure the local delivery notification options. Again, the default is appropriate in most instances.

The **Outbound Security** button is not normally used for Internet e-mail servers. Its purpose is to tell the SMTP server how to connect with other SMTP servers. The standard method is via anonymous access.

Clicking the **Outbound Connections** button opens the **Outbound Connections** window (Figure 8.13) that allows limits to be set on both the number of connections and connections per domain, as well as the timeout period. Unlike the settings on the **Messages** tab, these are hard limits. Once these limits are reached, additional connections will be refused. This screen also allows for the outbound **TCP port** to be changed from its default of port 25. Nearly all SMTP servers listen for incoming messages on port 25, so it is unlikely that this port setting will need to be changed.

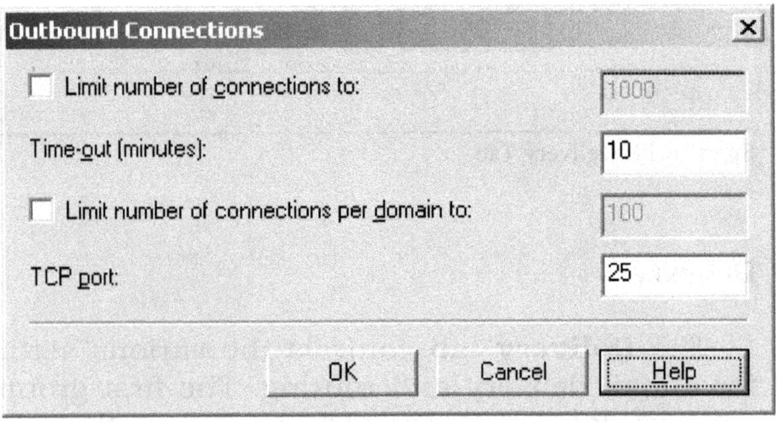

Outbound Connections		×
☐ Limit number of connections to:		1000
Time-out (minutes):		10
☐ Limit number of connections per domain to:		100
TCP port:		25
	OK Cancel Help	

Figure 8.13: Outbound Connections Window

The **Advanced** button under the **Delivery** tab is displayed in Figure 8.14. The **Maximum hop count** setting determines the maximum number of SMTP servers the message will be relayed to before being returned as undeliverable.

A domain name entered into the **Masquerade domain** field will automatically replace the domain name listed in the sender's e-mail address. For example, if the sender's e-mail address is listed in the message header as foo@mail3.foo.com, a masquerade domain of users.foo.com would change the 'From' address to read: foo@users.foo.com.

The **Fully-qualified domain name** filed is auto-populated by the virtual SMTP server and should correspond to the actual domain name that the server resides on.

The **Smart host** field lists the name of an alternative SMTP server that all mail should be routed to before it is returned. This setting is often used when a virtual SMTP server is behind a firewall, allowing the smart host to act as a gateway to the Internet. The smart host can be entered as a valid domain name, or as an IP address. However, if an IP address is used it must be enclosed in brackets, for example: [192.168.1.1].

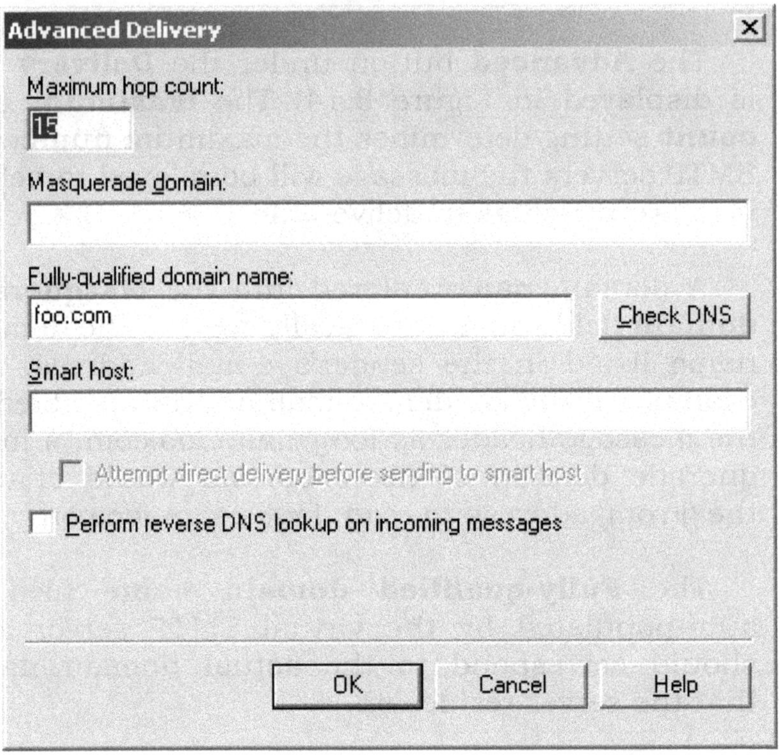

```
Advanced Delivery                                          [X]

Maximum hop count:
[15]

Masquerade domain:
[                                                        ]

Fully-qualified domain name:
[foo.com                                    ]  [Check DNS]

Smart host:
[                                                        ]

   [ ] Attempt direct delivery before sending to smart host

[ ] Perform reverse DNS lookup on incoming messages


                    [  OK  ]   [ Cancel ]   [  Help  ]
```

Figure 8.15: Advanced Delivery Option

The **Perform reverse DNS lookup on incoming messages** option will attempt to resolve the DNS name of any IP address from which the SMTP server receives e-mail. This option adds a performance hit each time it attempts a lookup and is not normally needed.

LDAP Routing

The **LDAP Routing** tab allows an SMTP server to communicate with Active Directory. Communicating with Active Directory will allow the SMTP server to resolve names of users who are members of Active Directory. Using LDAP allows the virtual SMTP server to resolve the name Nick Jones to the e-mail address nick.jones@foo.com provided, of course, that Nick Jones is an Active Directory user.

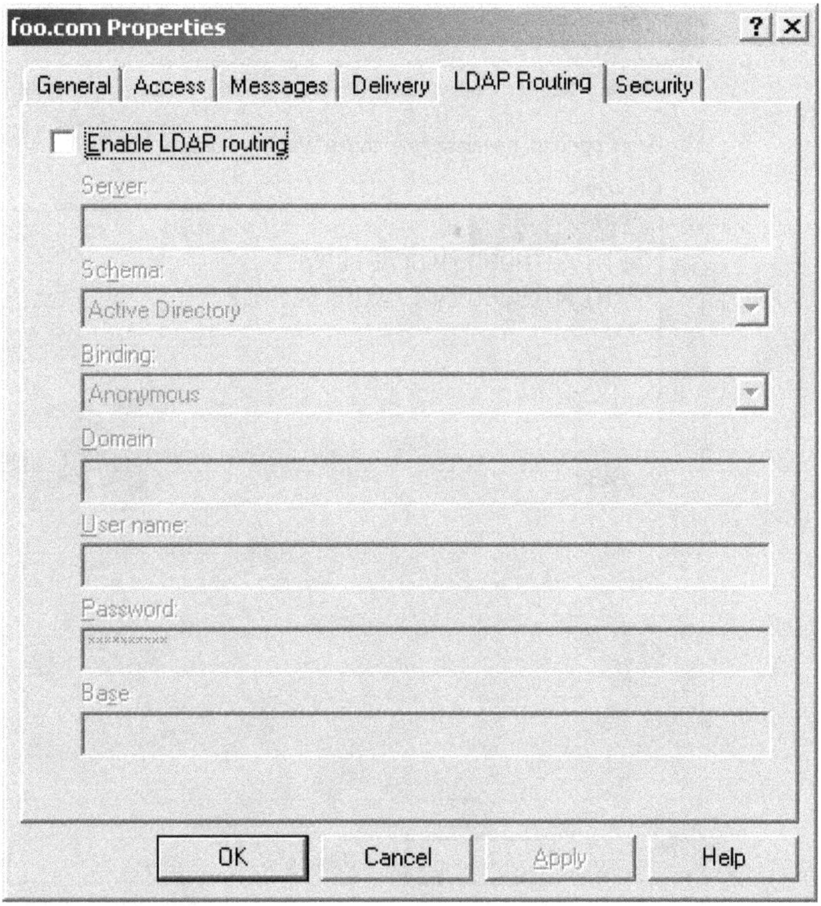

Figure 8.15: LDAP Routing

Security

Security is the final tab of the SMTP properties sheet (Figure 8.16). This tab allows for the addition or deletion of users or groups with access to modify this site's properties. The default administrators cannot be removed from this list.

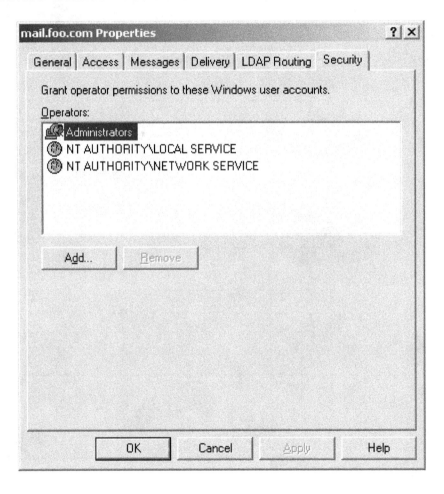

Figure 8.16: Security Tab

Summary

The SMTP Service provides a convenient and automated method for sending Internet e-mail. Although Virtual SMTP servers provide service for limited incoming e-mail, this cannot replace a true POP3 service as it does not deliver messages to each individual user's Inbox. The virtual SMTP server **Properties** window provides a centralized location for configuring the SMTP server's functionality.

Chapter 9

File Transfer Protocol (FTP) Service

FTP remains one of the most commonly used methods for copying files over the Internet. FTP's popularity can be attributed to several factors:

- FTP is a highly efficient protocol, with very little overhead, allowing for quick transfers.

- FTP is reliable, supporting both error checking and the resumption of failed downloads.

- FTP also has a large base of supporting client applications. There are FTP clients for Windows, most flavors of Unix, and Apple.

- Even more obscure operating systems like OS2, and BeeOS offer FTP clients. FTP is a practical protocol for transferring files over the Internet.

Overview

FTP is often used as a method for updating web pages. When a user logs in, he can be given access to the directory where web pages are stored and update and overwrite files as needed. These changes will automatically be reflected on the web site. This allows developers to update web sites from anywhere in the world. For example, a developer could be sitting in LaGuardia International airport, and get an urgent call from his manager about a pricing error that has been made on their website and must be corrected immediately. Using his PDA and a wireless access point the developer could update the web page with accurate pricing information in a matter of seconds.

All this convenience comes with a price, a high price; security. FTP is only capable of transferring passwords in clear text; encryption is not an option. This makes it very easy for a would-be hacker to monitor network traffic and sniff out the password, thereby granting the hacker full access to the entire website. Because of this major security concern, it is not generally recommended that FTP be configured with write access.

In enterprise networks FTP is often used as a download point for software repositories because it is more efficient than HTTP for transferring large files.

Getting Started

In Chapter 5, *Application and Website Configuration,* FTP was disabled as part of a security lockdown. To set up Microsoft FTP services the FTP Publishing Service will first need to be enabled via the **Publishing Services Properties** window (Figure 9.1) and the service will need to be started.

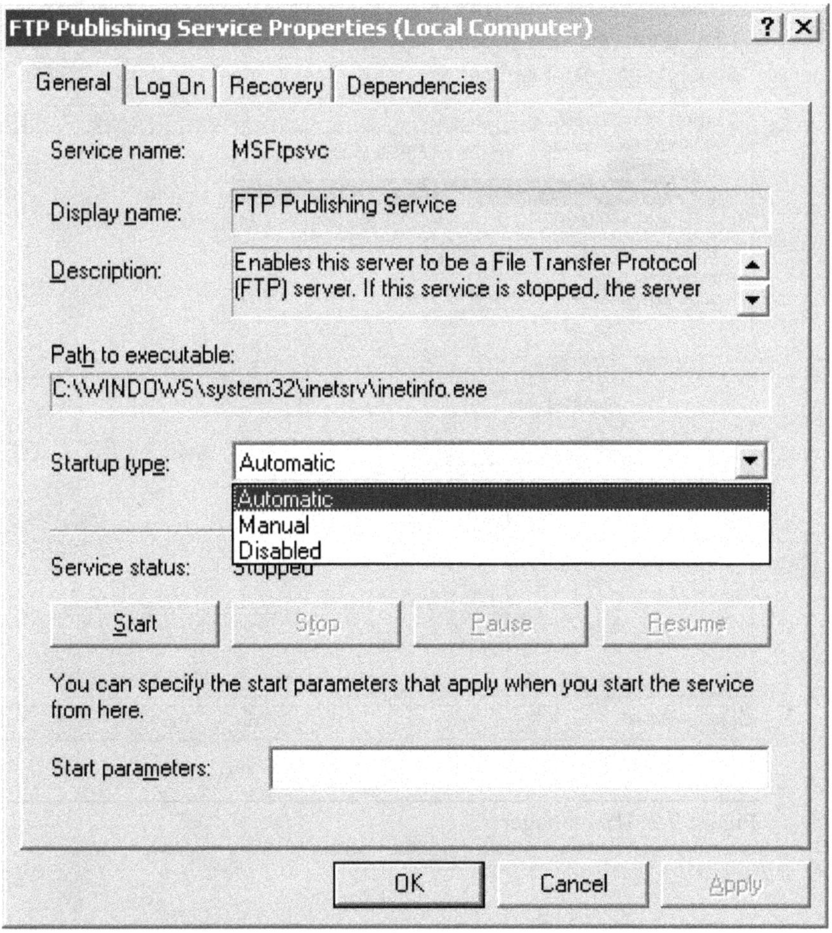

Figure 9.1 FTP Publishing Service Options

Once the FTP Publishing Service has been enabled, a new FTP site will need to be created via the IIS manager. If the FTP Sites folder has a red 'X' next to it, the FTP Publishing Service is not running, or is still disabled. Right-click the **FTP Sites** folder and select **New**, **FTP Site** (Figure 9.2). Also, note that FTP sites can be created from a file by selecting **FTP Site (from file)**.

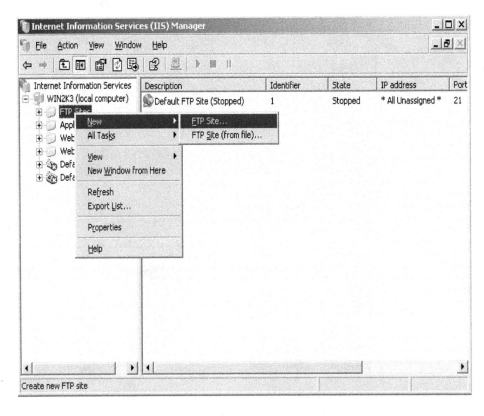

Figure 9.2: IIS manager

FTP Site Creation Wizard

The **FTP Site Creation Wizard** will open to assist with the creation of the new FTP site. Click **Next** at the first window. The next screen will prompt for a description of the FTP site (Figure 9.3). This description will be listed as the FTP folder name, so it is best to keep it short but descriptive.

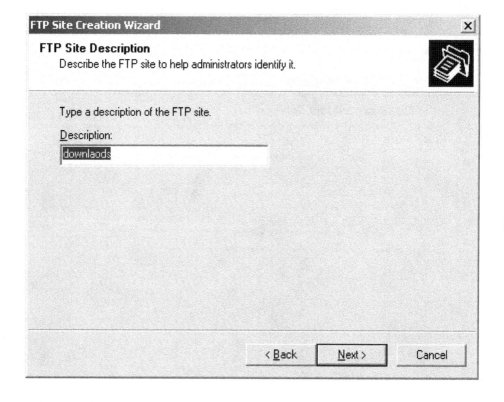

Figure 9.3: FTP Site Description

Clicking **Next** will bring up the **IP Address and Port Settings** window (Figure 9.4). Sites with only one IP address can leave the FTP site IP as **All Unassigned**. If the server has multiple IP addresses installed, select the appropriate IP address from the dropdown box. Next, select the **TCP port** number for FTP to use. Port 21 is the default port and is normally the appropriate port to select.

FTP does not support Host Header entries like HTTP/1.1, therefore each IP address can only have one FTP site running on each port. Client applications are configured by default to use port 21 so, if setting up multiple public FTP sites, it is advisable to set up multiple IP addresses per NIC and have each use port 21 with separate IP addresses.

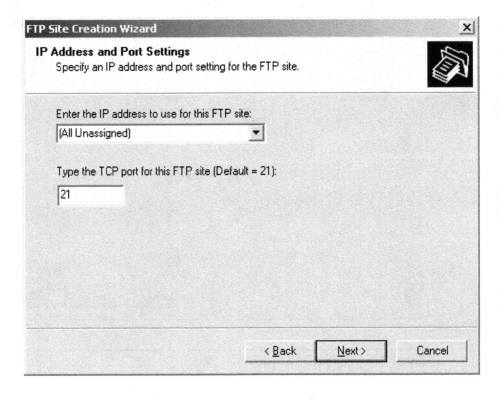

Figure 9.4 IP Address and Port Settings

User Isolation

The next screen configures **User Isolation** as shown in Figure 9.5. User Isolation restricts user access to individual home directories. This setting is a convenient way to set up separate isolated home directories for each user. There are three **User Isolation** settings:

1. Do not isolate users
2. Isolate users
3. Isolate users using Active Directory.

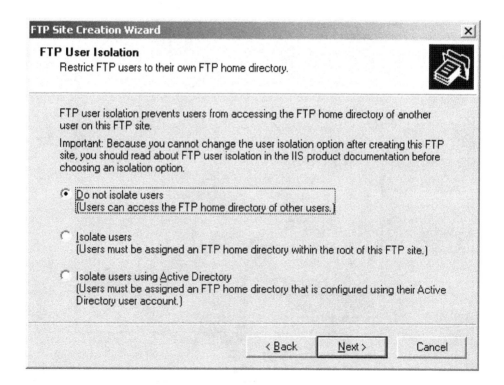

Figure 9.5: FTP User Isolation

The **Do not isolate users** setting effectively disables User Isolation, by not putting any home directory restrictions on users. **Isolate users** gives each user his or her own directory and restricts users from accessing any other directories or files. The **Isolate users using Active Directory** restricts users to the home directory specified in their Active Directory account.

In this example all users will connect to the FTP server using the same logon name, and will have access to the same folders. Select **Do not Isolate users** and click **Next**.

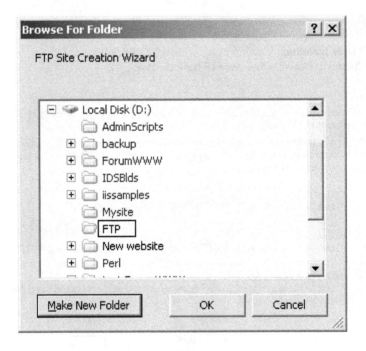

Figure 9.6: Browse for Folder

For this example we will setup the FTP root directory as d:\ftp. Hit **Browse**, expand the D drive and select **Make New Folder**. Rename the New Folder **FTP** (Figure 9.6) and click **OK**.

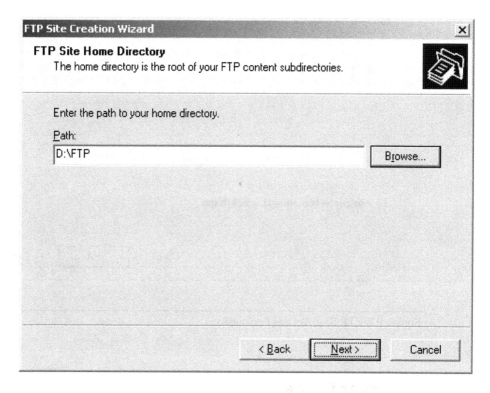

Figure 9.7 FTP Site Home Directory

Clicking **Next** will open the **FTP Site Access Permissions** window (Figure 9.8). Because this FTP site will be used for Anonymous downloads, select only **Read** access and click **Next**. This permission can be reconfigured at any time after the site is set up, as shown later in this chapter. Click **Finish** to close the wizard to complete installation of the new FTP site.

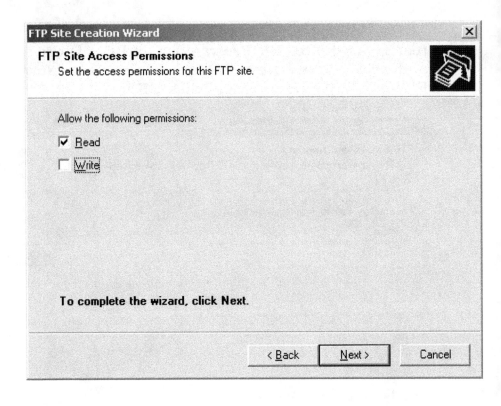

Figure 9.8 FTP Site Access Permissions

FTP Server Properties

The new FTP site should now be listed under the **FTP Sites** folder as **downloads**. Right-click the **downloads** FTP site and select **Properties** as shown in Figure 9.9.

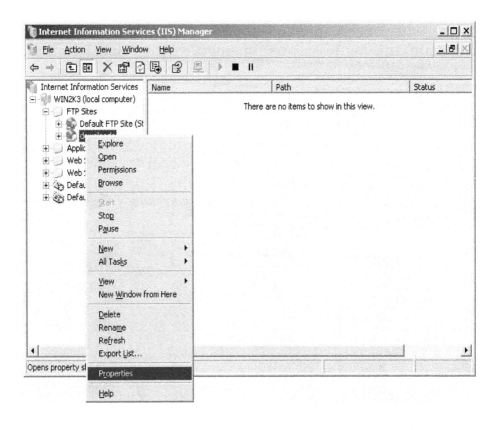

Figure 9.9: Selecting FTP Site Properties

FTP Site

This will open up the **Properties** window for the **downloads** website. The **FTP Site** tab (Figure 9.10) configures basic connectivity information. From this screen the FTP site name, IP address and TCP port can all be changed. Additionally, the number of connections for this site can be limited. If the server is not acting as a dedicated FTP server and will be running other applications (like IIS 6 web servers), it is recommended that a limit be placed on the number of user connections. This will prevent a flood of FTP users from connecting to the server, causing degraded service for other applications.

The **Connections limited to** field applies to the current FTP site only. If a server is set up with five FTP sites, each with connection limits of 1,000, it would be possible for 5,000 users to connect at once, 1,000 at each site. Global values can be created by selecting **Properties** for the **FTP Sites** root folder.

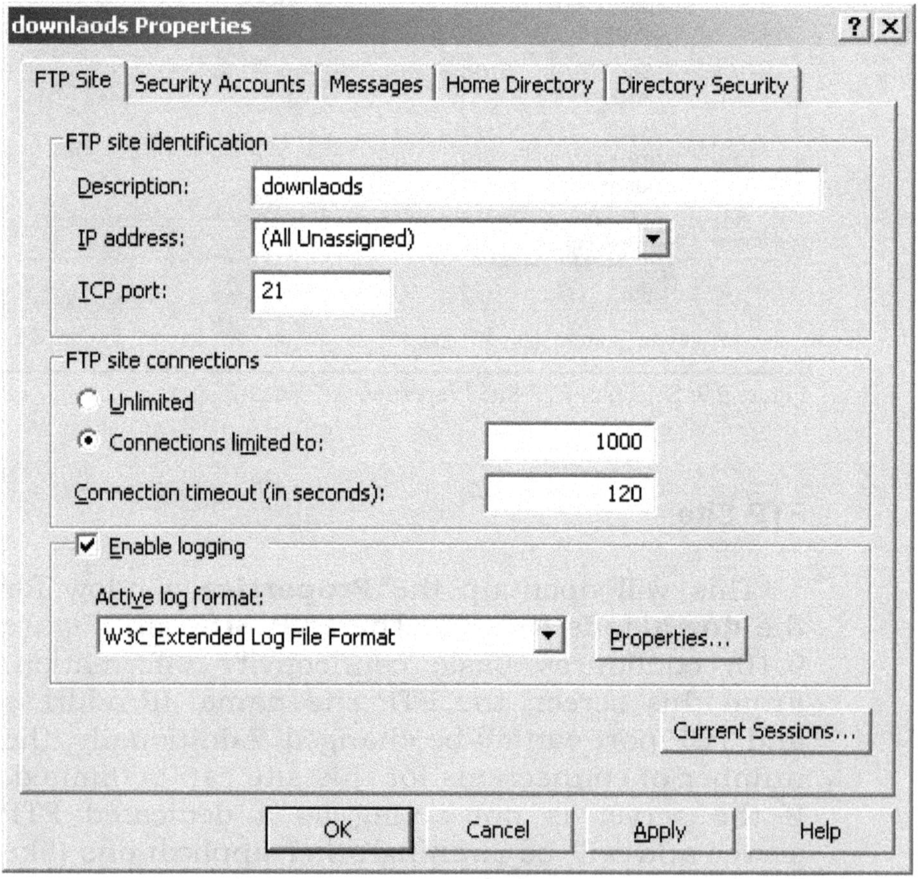

Figure 9.10: FTP site properties Tab

Security Accounts

The **Security Accounts** tab specifies if anony-mous connections are allowed. Security can be enhanced by renaming the account used for anonymous FTP access. Additionally, selecting **Allow only anonymous connections** will prevent users from connecting with privileged accounts.

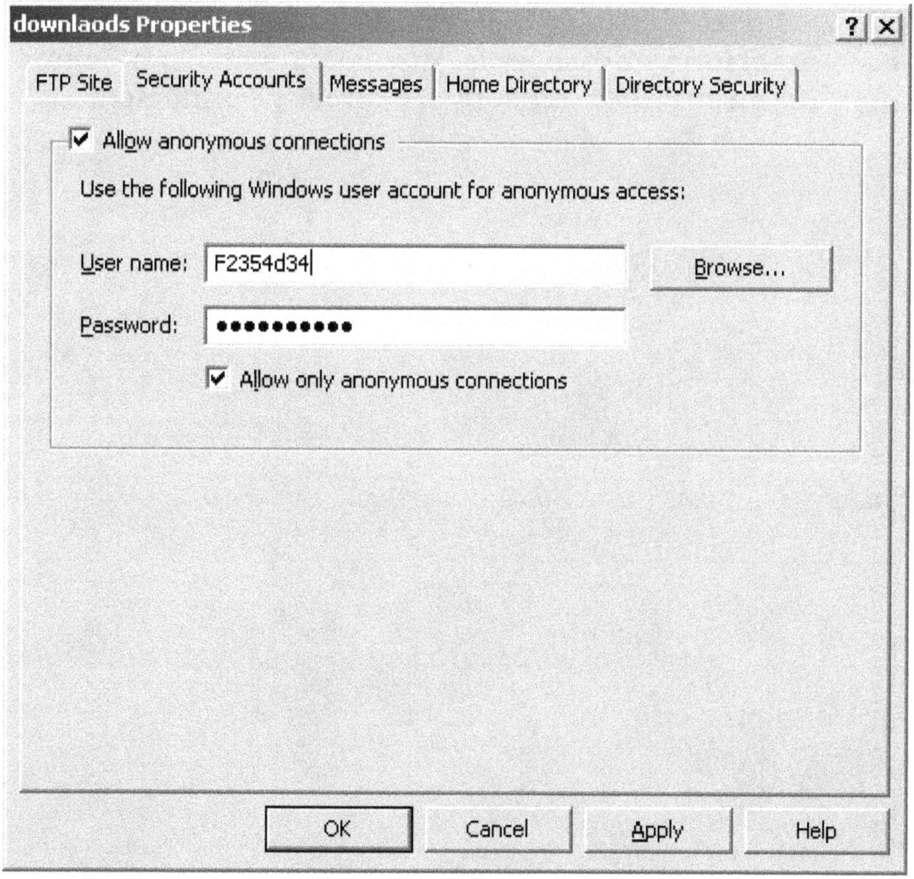

Figure 9.11: Security Accounts Tab

Messages

Figure 9.12 displays the **Messages** tab of the FTP **Properties** window. This tab configures messages that users will see when they log in. The **Banner** message is displayed anytime a user connects to the site, even if they are not granted access. The **Welcome** message is displayed on successful login. The **Exit** message is shown whenever a user logs out and the **Maximum connections** message is displayed when the maximum number of users are already connected.

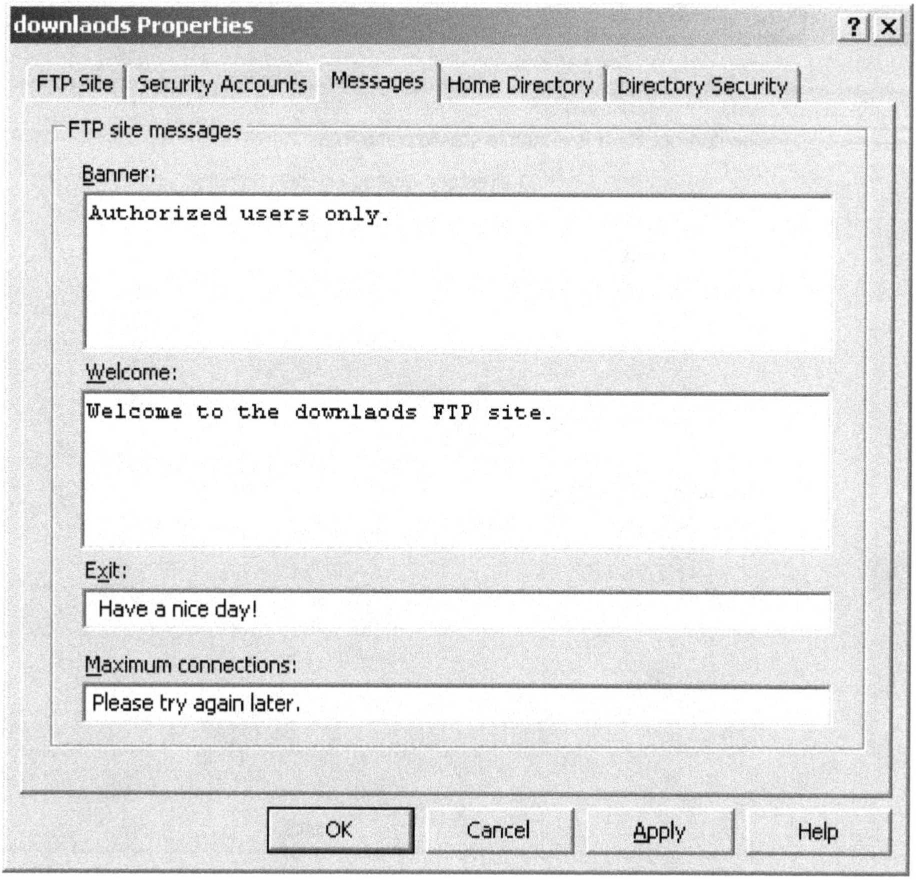

Figure 9.12 Messages Tab

Home Directory

The **Home Directory** tab, shown in Figure 9.13, can be used to reconfigure the home directory and access permissions for the site. Also, the directory listing type can be changed from MS-Dos to Unix in **Directory Listing Style**.

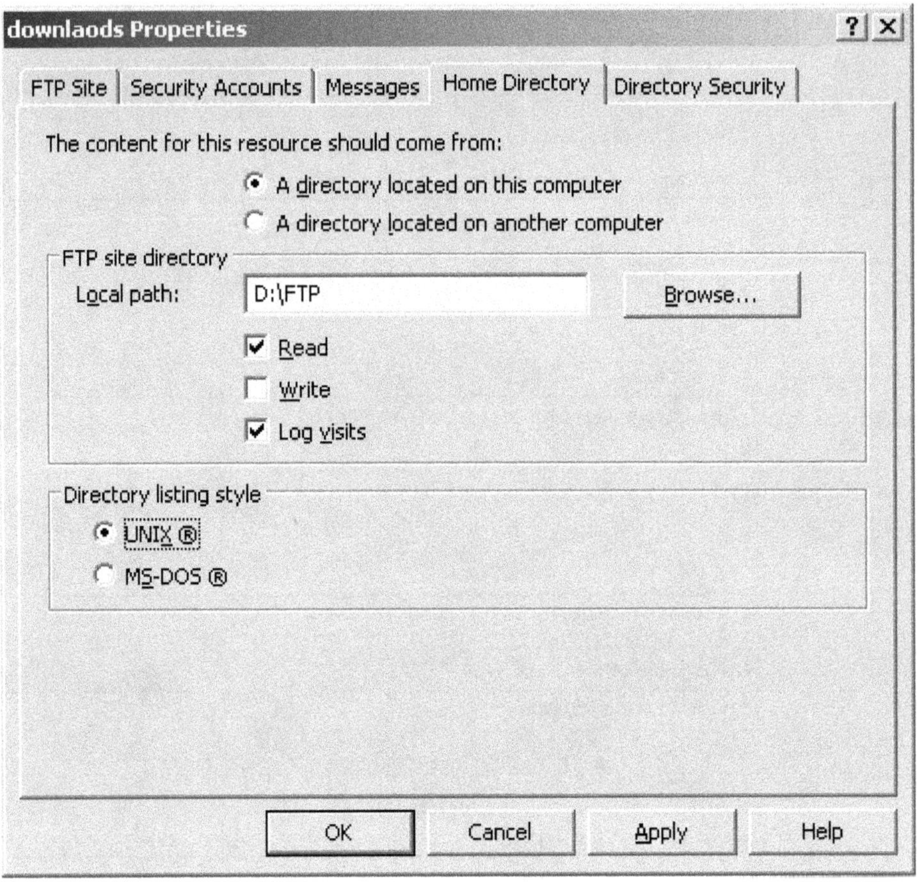

Figure 9.13: Home Directory Tab

Directory Security

The last tab, **Directory Security** (Figure 9.14), can be used to restrict access to ranges of IP addresses. These settings work like the IP address restrictions for IIS web sites. Multiple IP addresses can be allowed or restricted by including a subnet mask. A complete primer on subnet masks is beyond the scope of this book. However, specifying a default class C subnet mask will prohibit all users from the entire subnet. For example, specifying a network ID of 192.168.1.0 and a subnet mask of 255.255.255.0 will block all users from 192.168.1.1 to 192.168.1.254.

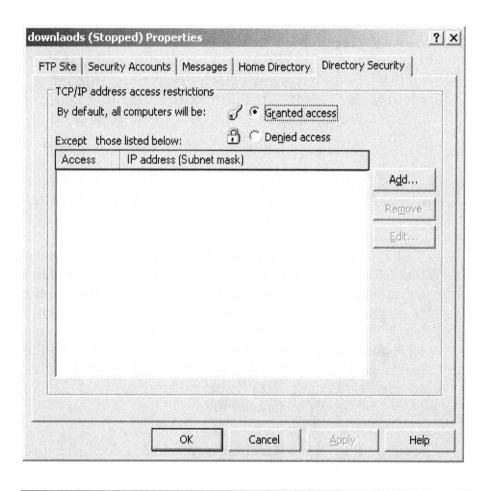

Figure 9.14: Directory Security Tab

Always remember to click **Apply** and test new settings. Now that the **downloads** site is configured and running, a final task is to copy any files that need to be made available for downloading.

Any files copied to the d:\FTP directory will be available for download, provided the FTP user account has been given read permission on that directory. By default, the **Everyone** account is often granted read access; this permission will allow anonymous users access to the file.

Summary

FTP is an extremely efficient and practical protocol for the transfer of files over the Internet. Due to passwords that can only be transferred in clear text, great care should be taken when implementing FTP. Specifically, it is often advisable to use FTP for read-only access. FTP should never be given access to systems, or important files or directories. Proper NTFS permissions must be in place for users to access files.

The **FTP Site Creation Wizard** simplifies the task of crating new FTP site. Once created FTP sites can be configured by right-clicking the FTP site and selecting the **Properties** option.

Chapter 10

Network News Transfer Protocol (NNTP) Service

The Network News Transfer Protocol (NNTP) provides a medium for posting and reading messages in a centralized forum open to anyone with Internet access. NNTP is commonly referred to as *newsgroups,* or *USENET news.*

NNTP Overview

Microsoft's implementation of NNTP that is provided with IIS 6.0 allows each virtual SMTP server to support separate configurations. Options allow different newsgroup subscriptions, anonymous or authenticated access, and event logging. Each virtual SMTP service sets up several subdirectories:

- Root – Each subscribed group will create a subdirectory under the root folders when news articles are kept. Newsgroups located within the hierarchy of the USENET server will be located in a similar file hierarchy. For example, the newsgroup alt.news.groups would be located under root/alt/news/groups.

- Pickup – Files placed in the Pickup directory are automatically moved to the Drop directory to be processed to the appropriate news groups. These articles must be properly formatted in order to be processed correctly.

- Drop – All incoming news articles are placed by the system in the Drop folder before being processed. This includes both local and remote news postings. Users should place postings in the Pickup directory, not directly in the Drop location.

- Failedpickup – All postings that cannot be processed are placed in this directory. This includes news postings with malformed headers.

- _slavegroup & _tempfiles_ – These are system files required for SMTP service operation. They are of no use to end users or administrators.

The NNTP service automatically subscribes to several default groups. These groups are used by the service and should not be unsubscribed.

Default subscribed groups:
- Control.cancel
- Control.newsgroups
- Control.rmgroup

Microsoft's NNTP service is designed to provide news service for a limited number of newsgroups as well as a limited number of users. This NNTP service is not suitable for providing a full news feed, or for supporting a large number of users.

New Virtual NNTP Server Wizard

To create a new virtual NNTP server, right-click on the default NNTP site and select **New**, **Virtual Server** as shown in Figure 10.1.

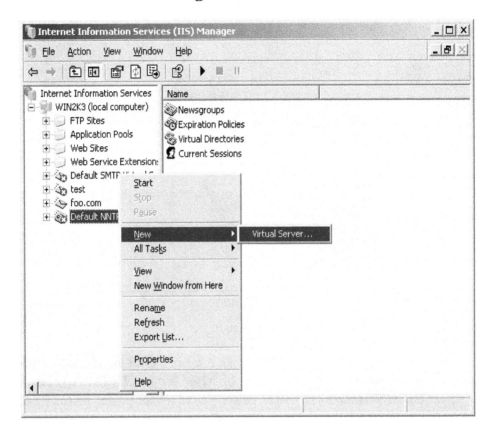

Figure 10.1: Creating a New NTP Server

This will start the **New NNTP Virtual Site Wizard**. The first screen prompts for the name of the virtual server. As stated in the previous chapter, the name should be short but descriptive. Enter an appropriate name and click **Next**.

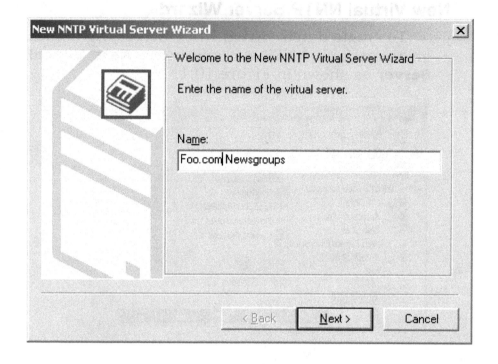

Figure 10.2: New NNTP Virtual Site Wizard

Figure 10.3 displays the **Select IP address and port number** window of the **New NNTP Virtual Site Wizard**. If multiple IP addresses are assigned on this server, select an IP address from the drop-down list. If only one IP address is available, or if only one NNTP server is going to be installed on the server, it is okay to leave the **All Unassigned** option selected.

Port 119 is the default port for NTP servers. Normally this should not be changed. Changing the port number can allow multiple virtual NNTP servers to be run on a single IP address, or provide increased security by making the NNTP service harder to locate.

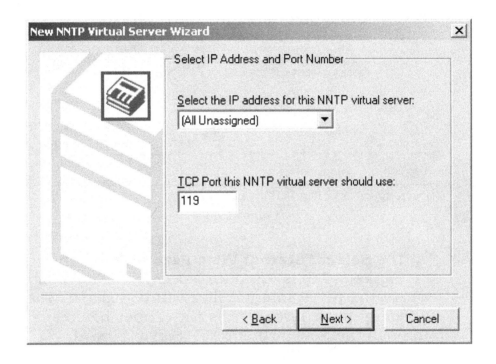

Figure 10.3: Select IP Address and Port Number

Like in the creation of the Virtual SMTP server, a port conflict message may be displayed. In this example, the default NNTP server is disabled, so ignore the error and select **Yes** (Figure 10.4).

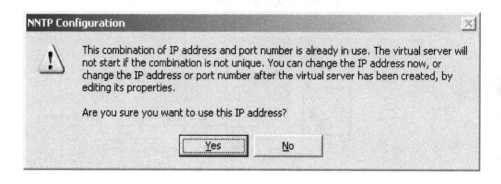

Figure 10.4: NNTP Port Verification Prompt

The **Select Internal Files Path** prompt, shown in Figure 10.5 is used to specify the directory where the NNTP internal files will be located. The directory must already exist; it cannot be created through the New Virtual NNTP Server Wizard.

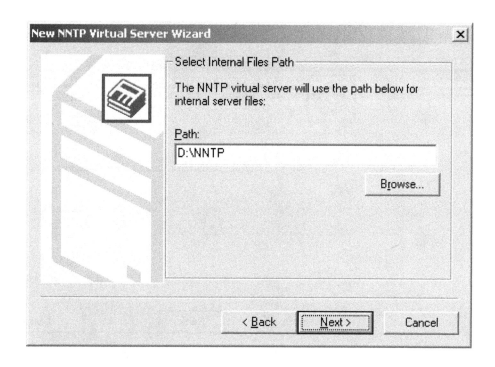

Figure 10.5: Internal Files Path

Clicking **Next** will allow the selection of either a local file system or a remote share to store the news content. Collectively, news files can take up a large amount of space, so it may be preferable to locate the news content on a remote share with a large amount of storage space.

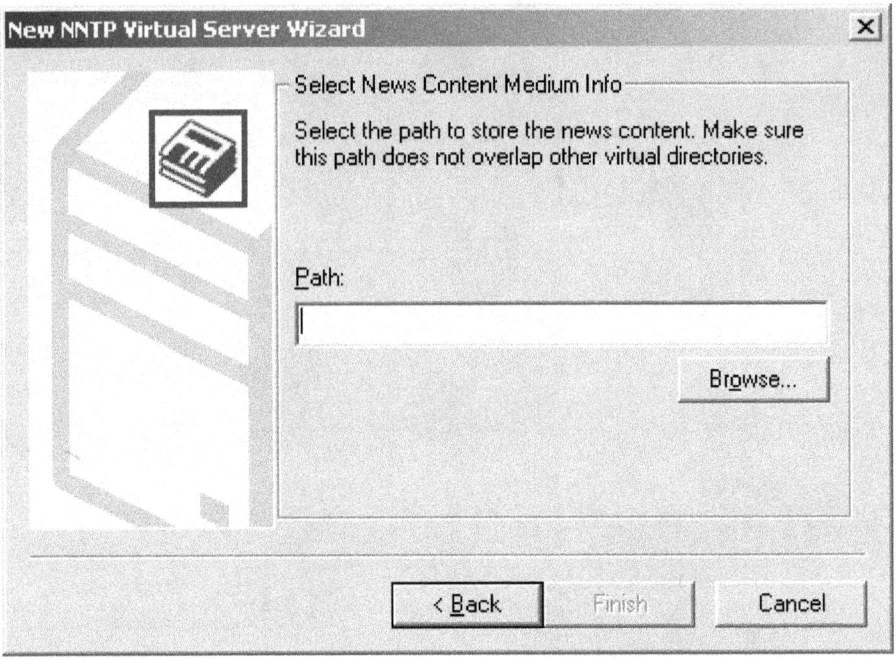

Figure 10.6: News Content Storage Directory

The last screen will prompt for the actual directory to be used to store the news articles. Any user who wishes to access SMTP services on this server will need to access this folder and its subdirectory. Whether the drive is local or a remote share, the path should be entered here (Figure 10.6). This directory must already exist on the server; it cannot be created through the New Virtual NNTP Server Wizard. Clicking **Finish** will create the new NNTP server.

NNTP Configuration

If the new NNTP server is not running, it can be started by right-clicking on the NNTP server's name and selecting **Start**. It may take several minutes to start the NNTP server. To configure the Virtual NNTP server, right-click the server's name and select **Properties**.

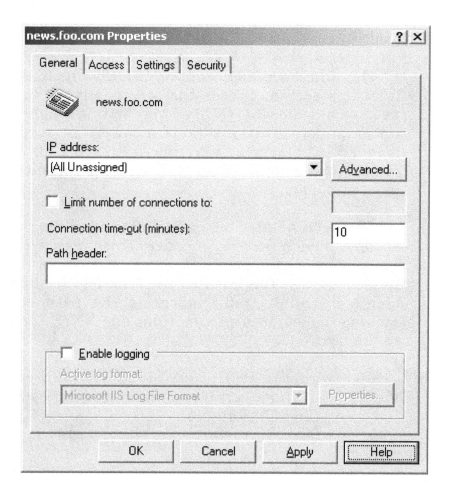

Figure 10.7: General Tab

General

The IP address can be changed from the **General** tab. Clicking on the **Advanced** button will allow the default NNTP port and secure NNTP port assignments to be changed.

The number of connections can also be limited from this screen. Unless the server is going to be used as a dedicated NNTP server, setting a limit on the number of connections allowed is recommended. The connection time-out is set to ten minutes by default, which should be sufficient for most implementations.

The **Path header** field adds a string to the path section of each message header. This creates a record on each message indicating that is has passed though this mail server. The feature helps create an audit trail, indicating the path each message takes as it passes from one NNTP server to the next.

Like with the HTTP and SMTP services, each virtual NNTP host can be configured to log events in several different formats.

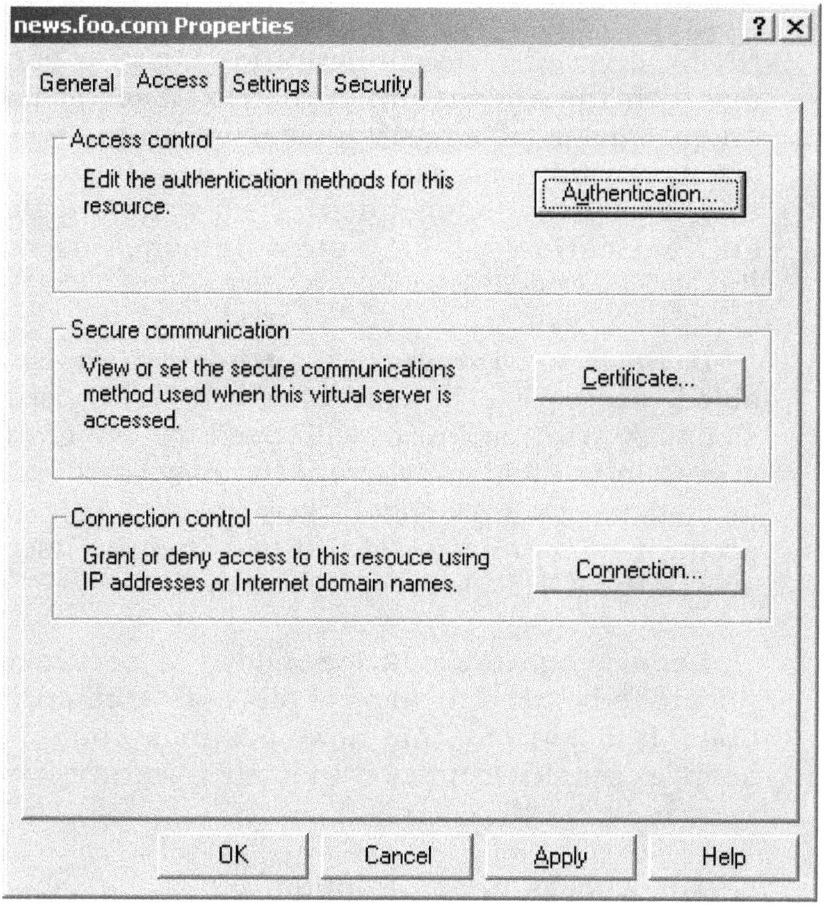

Figure 10.8 Access Tab

Access

If access is not properly configured, anyone on the Internet can use the NNTP service. Public news servers are in high demand. Allowing open access might result in a flood of Internet users monopolizing system resources.

To prevent unwanted users from accessing the NNTP server, several configuration changes can be made on the **Access** tab of the NNTP server properties. Clicking the **Authentication** button will allow anonymous access to be disabled. If practical, this is often recommended. Even enabling **Basic authentication** will keep most uninvited users off the NNTP service.

If **Basic** or **Integrated authorization** is enabled, access will be controlled via NTFS permissions. A user account will need to be granted access to the folders wherein the news articles are located (as well as the Pickup folder). This user account name and password can then be used to access the NNTP server.

Secure communication allows a secure certificate to be used to encrypt all NNTP communications. It is doubtful that news postings would be of such a sensitive nature that this feature would need to be used.

The **Access control** option works the same as the HTTP, SMTP or FTP programs. It can be set up to grant or deny access for an individual IP address, or a range of IP addresses. This is another setting that is vital in keeping unauthorized users off the server. When possible, provide a list or range of IP addresses to be granted access, and deny all others.

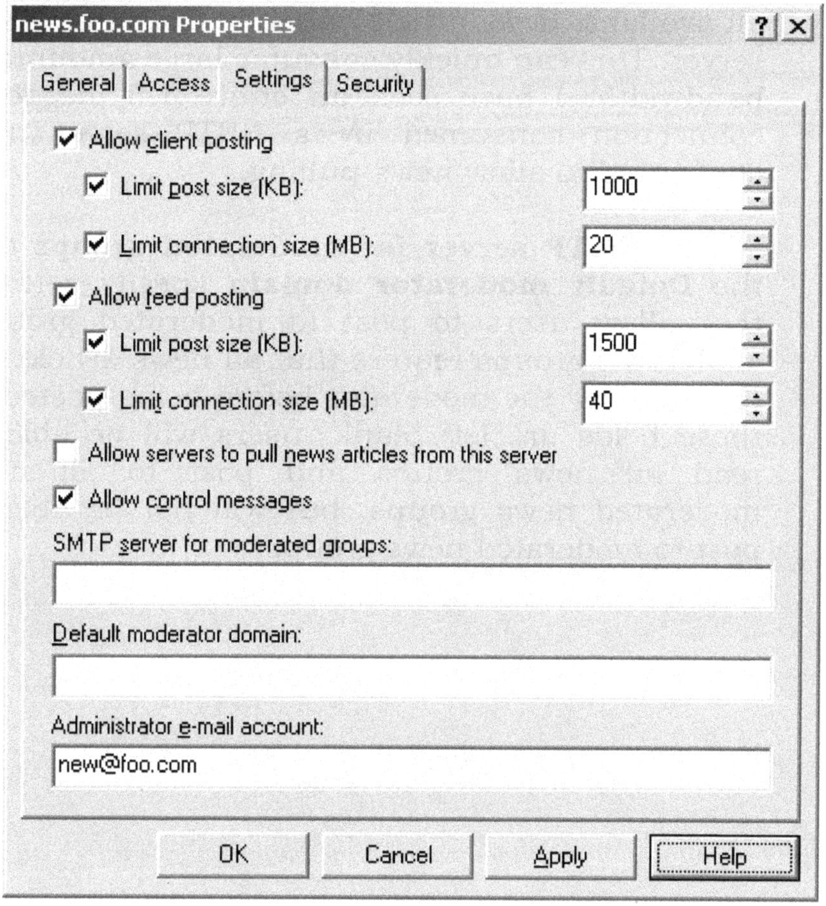

Figure 10.9: Settings Tab

Settings

The **Settings** tab configures message limits and properties. Settings such as limiting connection and message post size are configured here. Attention should be paid to the **Allow server to pull news articles from this server** option. If it is enabled, any server with access will be able to pull all available news articles directly from this NNTP server. This can quickly consume large amounts of bandwidth. I have seen an entire 1.5 megabyte connection consumed by a NNTP server mis-configured to allow news-pulling.

The **SMTP server for moderated groups** and the **Default moderator domain** specify settings that allow users to post to moderated groups. Moderated groups require that all news articles be approved by the moderator before being posted. If these fields are left blank, users will be able to read all news groups and post to all non-moderated news groups, but will not be able to post to moderated news groups.

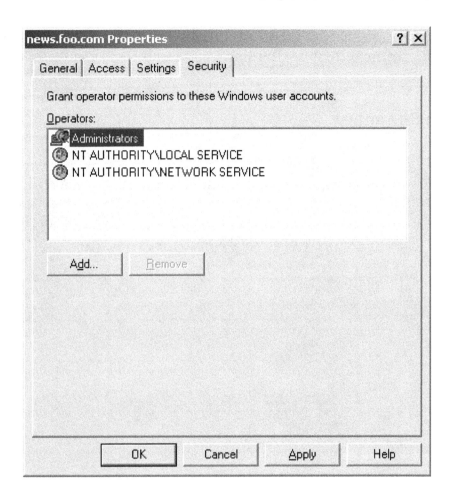

Figure 10.10: Security Tab

Security

Figure 10.10 displays the final tab of the NNTP properties screen, the **Security** tab. This tab allows for the addition or deletion of users or groups with access to modify this site's properties. Administrators, who are there by default, cannot be removed from this list.

Summary

Microsoft's NNTP Server provides rudimentary newsgroups read and post capabilities. Although short on features, it is easily configurable. Care must be taken to configure the NNTP server to disallow unwanted access.

Chapter 11

Microsoft Application Center Overview

The increase in the number of web servers using COM+ objects, such as the ones used with Active Server Pages (ASP), has made the task of keeping content on multiple web servers synchronized very difficult. The dynamic nature of today's web pages means that copying the content from one server to another using scripting is no longer a viable option for managing replication. This level of complexity requires that a manual process be used to synchronize both web and COM+ objects on multiple servers. While a manual process for synchronizing two web servers is less than ideal, when the number of servers that needs to be synchronized increases, the tasks can quickly become burdensome.

Microsoft's Application Center 2000 is designed to address the problems associated with managing web and COM+ objects on multiple servers by creating a web or application cluster. Application Center also simplifies scalability and reliability through the use of NLBS. Application Center is not part of IIS 6.0, but a separate product. As such, it requires separate purchase from the Windows Server 2003 product. Application Center 2000 SP1 will not run on Windows Server 2003. Application Center 2000 SP2 is required to install Application Center on all version of Windows Server 2003.

Application Center Features

NLBS is built into Application Center to provide scalability as well as guarantee reliability. NLBS is an integrated part of Application Center and therefore is automatically enabled at installation. If hardware load balancing is

Application Center Benefits

- **Scalability**

- **Reliability**

- **Manageability**

used, NLBS can be disabled by using the **Application Center New Cluster Wizard**.

NLBS allows for clusters of up to 32 servers, which can be added or removed dynamically. Reliability is achieved with automated failover; the cluster can continue to process requests even if multiple members of a cluster fail simultaneously. The monitoring tools that are provided with Application Center detect hardware and software failures automatically and can trigger actions, such as running scripts or sending e-mail notification, in response to failures. For a more detailed look at NLBS see Chapter 6: *Network Load Balancing.*

Application Center provides a custom interface for NLBS, allowing you to access the NLBS settings via a convenient and simplified interface. This interface includes all the standard options commonly needed when creating an Application Center cluster. If more control is needed over NLBS, the main **NLBS Control Panel**, located under the **Network Properties** dialog box, can also be used to customize the settings.

Management

Application Center uses the intuitive and standardized Microsoft Management Console. This console simplifies the tasks of network and component load balancing, managing replication, as well as monitoring web and COM+ objects. The **Application Center Management Console** can be installed on client machines, allowing for convenient remote administration. Application Center also provides easy to use wizards, which not only guide administrators through the installation process, but also check for hardware and software dependencies. Command-line and browser-based management tools provide easy administration and flexibility by allowing the cluster to be administered from anywhere.

Component Load Balancing

Component Load Balancing (CLB) is the Application Center service that allows COM objects to be load balanced among the members of a cluster. CLB requires substantial CPU overhead and therefore careful consideration should be given to determine its suitability for a given network. CLB is best suited for environments that rely heavily on COM objects, or where COM servers need to be isolated for increased security. Itanium 2 and Xeon servers are well equipped to handle the additional CPU overhead that CLB requires and can be an excellent choice when implementing CLB.

> *We originally selected Application Center because it enabled component load balancing across the business logic tier of our systems. After working with it, we've come to recognize the benefits provided by its many other features including integration with Network Load Balancing, Cluster Health Monitoring, and Replication. It makes managing entire clusters as simple as administering a single computer.*
>
> —Justin Mette
>
> Consulting Engineer
> Galileo International

Application Center is not only invaluable for web servers; it can also provide failover and load balancing while simplifying the management of non-web applications. Thick-client applications, such as Visual Basic programs, can leverage Application Center regardless of whether they use HTTP or DCOM to communicate.

Application Center Operation

Application Center is designed to make website and application management simple and auto- mated. Separate solutions are often developed to address the issues of server configuration, content publishing, replication, and monitoring. Applica- tion Center provides a single, complete solution for these issues.

Application Center defines one member of a cluster as the cluster controller. The settings and content on this controller are replicated out to every member of the cluster. Application Center not only synchronizes web and application con- tent, it also maintains a consistent set of applica- tion and server settings across the entire cluster.

Network related information such as port rules, client affinity, and NIC settings are all automati- cally copied from the cluster controller to each member of the cluster. The cluster controller also maintains cluster management settings, such as cluster name, cluster accounts and passwords, as well as other cluster settings. As discussed earlier, web and COM+ objects such as HTML, XML, and ASP's are also automatically replicated from the cluster controller. This complete automated man- agement saves a considerable amount of time for system administrators.

The job of keeping content on multiple servers synchronized is labor-intensive and time- consuming. Developers may need to update web- sites several times a day or more. Administrators often give in and just provide developers administrative access on the web servers, which can lead to additional problems later on. Application Center automatically replicates content to all members of the cluster, eliminating the need to give developers full administrative control of the entire cluster. Instead, they can be given just the access needed to update content on the cluster controller. Content automation can also eliminate the need for a staging server that acts like a central push point for new code.

Defining an Application

Under Application Center, an *application* is defined as the content and software for either a web site, a COM+ application or both. Many administrators generally refer to this generically as "the website". However, we are talking about not only the content, but also certificates, registry keys, and settings. An application can contain more than one website or COM+ application and it will still be treated as one logical unit by the cluster.

To define an application, use the **Application View**. The Application View is where you identify the content and resources that make up the application. The Application View is similar to a simplified version of the MMC snap-in for website management. By using the Application View, a default application or several custom application definitions can be created.

The resource types that can be configured as part of application definition include:

- COM+ applications
- Data source names
- File system variables
- Registry keys
- Web sites and virtual directories

Application Deployment and Synchronization

When an application is defined and ready to go online Microsoft simplifies the process with the **New Deployment Wizard**. The New Deployment Wizard identifies the cluster controller, member servers, applications, and configuration options to deploy to each member of the cluster.

Application Center is capable of synchronizing all of the following information:

- COM+ applications
- Web content
- Active Server pages
- Virtual web sites
- ISAPI filters
- Files and directories
- Crypto API server certificates
- Metabase configuration information
- Registry keys
- System data source names
- Application Center Windows Management Instrumentation (WMI)

The pre-configured setting for Application Center is to synchronize the cluster once every 60 minutes. Additionally, any time new content is added to the cluster controller, or its settings are changed, a partial synchronization is preformed to provide all members with the updated data. In the **Application View**, the cluster can be synchronized at any time by clicking the **Synchronize** button located on the Application View toolbar.

Cluster Health and Monitoring

Microsoft's Application Center provides robust monitoring, performance, and health statistics. Application Center's monitoring is so complete, it is doubtful that a third party monitoring solution would be needed to maintain production stability. The **New Cluster Wizard** automatically configures Application Center to e-mail alerts to an administrative account using a standard SMTP server. Application Center logs important events to the Windows event log. Additionally, Application Center's monitoring is integrated with Microsoft's Operations Manager (MOM).

Category	Major Counters
Web Service	Thread Count, Request execution time, Request wait time
System	Page reads/sec, Interrupts/sec, Processor queue length, %DPC time
SQL Server	% Disk time, Total server memory, Buffer cache hit ratio, Number of deadlocks/sec
COM Objects	Total committed transactions, Object Creations/sec, Timeout shutdown
Miscellaneous	Process: Thread count, NIC: bytes sent/sec, Bytes sent/sec

Table 11.1 Application Center Counter

Application Center provides myriad counters for networks, servers, and applications, as seen in Table 11.1. Statistics are updated in real-time and historical data can be displayed every 15 minutes, hourly, daily, weekly, or even in quarterly increments. This flexibility in presenting historical data provides the information necessary for trending and capacity planning.

Application Center's health monitoring console includes performance counters for both the entire cluster and individual cluster members. These local and global counters will alert administrators before a cluster or cluster member reaches capacity. The monitoring console allows for easy configuration of custom monitors and alerts.

High Powered Servers and Application Center

We have already mentioned the advantages of using high-end servers for serving COM+ objects.

COM+ objects can be very powerful and have potential for misuse. Therefore, organizations often
opt to place them behind a firewall. Figure 11.1
displays the basic architecture for this type of configuration. A cluster of two Xeon servers located
behind a firewall are used to deliver COM+ objects,
while a cluster of Pentium servers deliver all web
content. This configuration is ideal for delivery of a
secure and robust application solution.

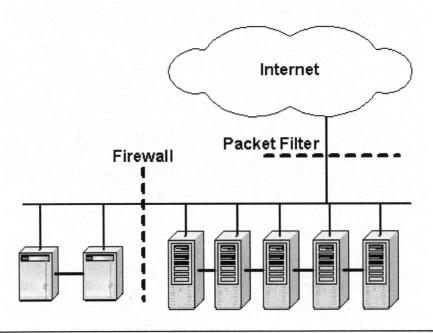

Figure 11.1: High Powered Web Solution

Adding a high-end server and Application Center to an existing web farm allows a system engineer to realize the benefits of the increased power
and flexibility, as well as Application Center's performance and failover capabilities.

When converting an existing web farm from
several separate pools of web servers to one or

more Application Center cluster, it is critical to understand the existing environment's configuration and dependencies. Often, due to company policies or network requirements, it is not possible or desirable to convert your entire web farm into a single cluster. Separating web clusters into logical groups can still provide simplified administration and management.

Retiring several out-of-date web servers is an ideal time to replace these older servers with a single high-end Xeon-based server. This gives the benefit of not having to replace all the web servers in your current environment, but still enables an organization to take advantage of the benefits that come with using Itanium and Application Center.

Often, as websites need additional capacity, overworked servers are simply replaced with more powerful servers. This requires an upgrade project, which usually includes backup and manual transfer of data, as well as downtime and scheduling of application maintenance windows.

Once the new servers are tested and brought online the older servers are often donated to charity, or used for development work. This typical upgrade path results in zero failover and a large administrative overhead to manage each website separately. However, if an organization decides to create a single cluster using just one server, they can continue to utilize their existing web servers and gain failover for all their websites.

In Figure 11.2 shows how this is accomplished with a two-stage implementation. First, the new server is configured as a single-node cluster. Then the content and settings from each of the existing corporate websites can be integrated into this cluster. Once this cluster is completed, testing is done to insure correct functionality. The older web servers are taken offline and the cluster assumes production service.

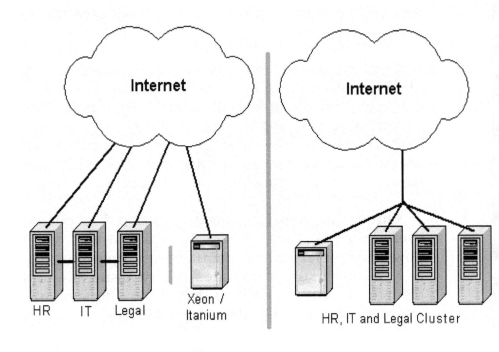

Figure 11.2 High Powered Webfarm

It is then an easy process to reuse the remaining servers for failover and load balancing. This is a great time to rebuild the servers with the latest operating systems and service packs, as this will usually improve system stability. Once these servers have been rebuilt and Application Center has been installed, the Application Center New Member Wizard will automatically add these servers to the cluster and then automatically copy the current settings and content to each new member.

Be sure to assign these members a lower load weight value than the new, more powerful server was assigned, so the new server will receive the bulk of user requests. If these servers are to be used only in case of a failure of the main server, give then a load weight of 1 so that they will only receive requests if the primary server goes offline or is unable to process additional requests.

Clustering Scenarios

Microsoft Application Center supports three primary clustering scenarios. This section provides general information for each of these primary clustering scenarios.

- **Single-Node Cluster**
- **Standard Web Cluster**
- **COM+ Application Cluster**

Single-Node Cluster

It can be useful to operate Application Center on a single server, without any other cluster members. Application Center treats a single-node cluster, or stand-alone server, as a cluster of one member. The most common single-node cluster is a 'stager', or staging server. A staging server is used as a place to load content before it goes onto the production servers. This staging server allows for experimenting with and full testing of the quality and functionality of content from development and test environments before deploying the content to production environments.

In addition to staging servers, other single-node clusters can benefit from Application Center without operating in a clustered environment. These servers can use Application Center for such tasks as:

- Deploying applications to or from other members or clusters.
- Viewing health and status of other clusters.
- Viewing performance data and event logs from other clusters.

Standard Web Cluster

The most common Application Center clustering scenario is a Web cluster serving web sites and local COM+ components. Such clusters should be distinguished by whether they use NLBS or another type of load balancing device. The advantages of clustering multiple servers together include:

- Failover protection— each cluster member is essentially a backup of the cluster controller.

- Increased application availability— with multiple members serving sites and applications, clients can experience uninterrupted service regardless of failures or problems on individual members.

- Increased scalability— members can be added or removed without affecting cluster availability.

- Increased performance— client workload is distributed throughout the cluster, so that each individual member receives lesser load, which in turn enhances performance.

While the advantages of using clusters are numerous, the tasks generally associated with cluster administration can often become complex and labor intensive. Application Center simplifies many of these tasks and provides the following capabilities:

- Quick setup and configuration of clusters— the New Cluster Wizard simplifies the process of creating a cluster.

- Simplified cluster administration— manage multiple cluster members from a single computer, even remotely.

- Seamless integration with NLBS— Application Center can be used to configure and manage NLBS.

- Cluster synchronization— synchronize all members by setting an interval for periodic synchronization or by manually initiating synchronization (this includes synchronizing server configuration, application content, application configuration, and network settings for NLBS).

- CLB capabilities—load balance components for COM+ applications and process COM+ applications on designated application servers.

- Simplified application deployment— by using the Deployment Wizard to deploy applications.

- Monitoring capabilities—view the health of and performance for members, applications, and clusters.

- Automation of administrative tasks— use Application Center monitors and the command-line tool for automating common administrative tasks, such as restarting services or setting members offline.

NLBS Web Clusters

Application Center provides seamless integration with NLBS. Cluster creation and member addition is simplified and common administrative tasks, such as setting members online and offline, can be handled through the Application Center user interface. NLBS dynamically distributes client workload as members are set online and offline. Figure 11.3 shows a typical one-tier web cluster that is running NLBS.

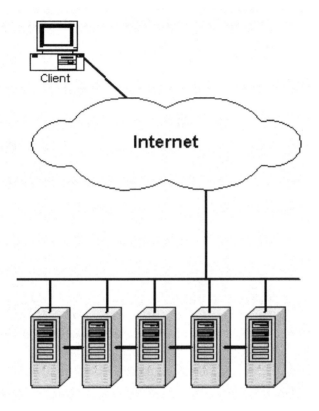

Figure 11.3: NLBS Web Cluster

To increase performance and availability, simply add members to the cluster by using the **Add Cluster Member Wizard**.

Non-NLBS Web Clusters

For non-NLBS clusters, an external load-balancing device, such as Cisco's Local Director, is used to distribute incoming client requests.

To create a cluster that uses an external load-balancing device, in the **New Cluster Wizard**, select **Other load balancing**. This will disable NLBS. For further information about third-party load balancing integration, see the *Microsoft Application Center 2000 Resource Kit.*

COM+ Application Cluster

A COM+ application cluster processes COM+ application requests for clients. These clients can include Windows-based clients and Web clusters. A COM+ application cluster relieves Web clusters and Windows-based clients from processing COM+ components. To support Windows-based clients by using DCOM, the cluster can use NLBS or other load balancers to distribute incoming client requests.

You can create Web clusters that use CLB to load balance the activation requests for COM+ components and forward these requests from the Web cluster to the COM+ application cluster for processing. In a two-tier Application Center clustering environment, one tier handles requests for Web sites while the second tier handles requests for COM+ components. The performance for this environment may not match the performance of a single Web cluster because data must be transmitted between the Web cluster and COM+ application cluster. While the best performance is achieved by activating COM+ applications locally, creating a separate cluster to process COM+ components has the following advantages:

- Increased security because you can place firewalls between Web clusters and COM+ application clusters so that clients accessing the Web cluster are restricted from accessing the COM+ application cluster.

■ If the COM+ applications consume extensive processing resources, Web servers may become unresponsive. You can create a separate COM+ application cluster to relieve the Web cluster from processing these COM+ applications. Since the Web cluster does not process the COM+ applications, it can achieve better performance in serving websites.

■ Increased manageability of server applications because COM+ applications are isolated on a separate cluster from Web clusters. The two separate clusters allow you to have different developers and administrators maintaining each cluster independently.

■ Support for clients of mixed environments; COM+ application clusters can accept requests from both clients accessing the Web cluster and clients running Windows-based applications.

To configure a two-tier Application Center cluster where one tier handles requests for Web sites and another tier processes COM+ components, you must complete the following steps:

1. Create a Web cluster and a COM+ application cluster.
2. Install the COM+ applications on both clusters.
3. On the Web cluster:

    ■ Use the Component Services snap-in to enable dynamic load balancing support for the components you want load balanced by CLB.

    ■ Restart the COM+ component load balancing service.

    ■ Configure the COM+ routing list to include each of the members comprising the COM+ application cluster.

4. On the COM+ application cluster, disable dynamic load balancing support for each component.

As clients send activation requests for COM+ components, the Web cluster determines if the components support dynamic load balancing and if so, forwards the request to one of the COM+ application cluster members on the routing list.

Summary

Microsoft's Application Center simplifies the administration of enterprise class websites, while giving administrators increased flexibility. Application Center provides content management, load balancing, and failover.

Although not appropriate for every web application, CLB offloads CPU intensive web components to a high –end server or cluster of servers. High-end Intel-based servers can be teamed with CLB to allow for a robust and secure front-end application.

Chapter 12

Securing the Server

While security has always been an important consideration for any large enterprise, the recent proliferation of fast spreading viruses and trojans has caused an increased spotlight on server security. This is particularly true for web servers, as many exploits target vulnerabilities in IIS.

Today it would be almost unheard of to connect a private network to the Internet without the use of a firewall. However, many companies don't have a centralized virus management system, service pack and security patch rollout process, or even a security threat response plan.

Server Level Security

In the past, the lion's share of attention was given to securing the network, while individual servers (and clients) have been widely ignored. The Code Red and NIMDA virus outbreaks showed corporate America just how susceptible individual servers are once a trojan gets inside the network.

Firewalls offer little, if any, protection once even a single system on the network is infected. Both operating system vendors and virus software companies such as Microsoft and Symantec usually address these trojans by having patches available within hours of a widespread breakout. The problem is that most companies do not have the procedures and infrastructure needed to deploy these fixes in a timely manner. Web servers are particularly susceptible to security threats from the Internet, because they, by design, provide access to the entire Internet.

Firewalls and traffic filtering are critical to secure a network, regardless of its size. While traffic filtering is outside of the scope of this book, this chapter should not be construed to endorse a replacement for conventional traffic filtering hardware. A comprehensive security plan includes procedures for securing both the network and the servers; securing only one leaves major security gaps. A firewall can be compared to a protective garment, like latex gloves or an organic respirator; they are worn outside of body and are a first line of protection. Patches and virus software can be compared to antibiotics and vaccines, which are administered intravenously. They protect the body from the inside after a virus has invaded.

A well thought-out security plan should include preventative measures, compliance and proactive monitoring, eradication procedures and policies, as well as disaster recovery procedures. The plan must be structured, yet flexible enough to allow for change and improvement. Input from all levels of employees should be taken into consideration during the planning and day-to-day operation. Managers and CIOs can devise security policies and procedures that look great on paper, but without input from technical professionals, they rarely perform as well as planned.

Preventing Attacks

There are two critical factors to take into account when planning preventive procedures. First, there are virus patches. A well-deployed virus solution can mean the difference between deploying the latest virus patch in a matter of minutes, rather than a matter of days. Secondly, security fixes must be proactively installed when new threats are discovered. After some criticism for complacency, Microsoft has stepped up its security patch efforts, resulting in myriads of patches that seem to be released on a regular basis.

Virus Patches

An effective virus solution should be almost completely automated so that it requires little, if any, administrator intervention for daily operation. Products such as Norton Antivirus Corporate Edition© allows automated server scanning and virus definition updates. They can be configured to automatically delete or quarantine infected files and even send automatic e-mail or pager notification.

In the event of a new virus outbreak, the updated definition only needs to be applied to the central virus server, which then pushes the definition to all servers. IT departments that have centralized anti-virus servers and documented procedures can respond to major virus outbreaks in a matter of hours. Conversely, other departments without a centralized solution work around the clock for several days, manually updating and scanning each server. The return on investment (ROI) for a centralized virus console can not only be measured in man hours saved, but in potential loss of income that an averted downtime would have caused. However ROI is measured, it is easy to see the value of a centralized virus solution for all but the smallest IT organization.

Security Patches

Both Unix and Microsoft servers need to keep up-to-date with the latest patches. Being attacked by a security exploit that was fixed by a patch released several months ago can be hazardous to one's employment. However, manually installing every patch on every server as they are released can quickly become hazardous to one's personal life.

A middle ground must be found. It is typically not economically feasible to patch every server as new security patches are released. Yet, waiting for a major server pack to be released opens a network to an unreasonable risk of attack.

By defining criteria that can be used to measure the amount of risk each new security patch addresses priority can more easily be identified. These criteria are unique for every network, but the factors to be considered commonly include risk exposure: is an exploit currently available, and is the threat or attack active? Having a panel of experts with different job roles is critical for proper risk assessment. Managers, security experts, integrators, network and server personnel should all be included on this panel.

Patch Deployment

The next hurdle to tackle is how to test and deploy security patches. Small IT departments can simply keep a test bed of servers on which to test out new patches. Enterprise networks, on the other hand, simply have too many applications and custom configurations to test each patch on every platform. One solution is to have a global engineering or architecture group test and validate each patch on the most commonly used platforms and applications. Then, let each individual group conduct limited testing on their custom applications. Ultimately, each organization must strike a balance between the risk of introducing an issue on a server and the amount of time spent testing patches.

Unlike virus monitoring there are no complete security patching solutions. Several companies are working on products to address this need. However, most are new and lack the functionality a large enterprise requires. An organization has two main choices on how to deploy patches, centralized or distributed.

Some organizations have opted to develop their own in-house applications for centralized patch deployment, while others are using Microsoft SMS. IT organizations that provide a broad range of services may find that centralized security patch deployment do not fit their innumerable application configurations. Still, many are patching each server by hand, a time-consuming effort.

Distributed Patch Deployment

A centralized patch deployment solution is not flexible enough to meet the needs of most large IT organizations. The rest of this chapter will focus on effectively using a distributed virus patch process. If well planned and used effectively, a distributed patch process can provide a secure computing environment for even a very large and complex network.

Often, companies that use a centralized patch process believe that, by pushing patches to every server, they have protected their entire environment. What they may fail to address is servers that fall though the cracks. Often the push, or the patch application process fails. Centralized reporting of an entire network is not viable since it often causes unacceptable levels of network congestion. This can be very difficult to manage and often provides erroneous reports.

In a decentralized patch deployment solution, reporting is done at a group level. This reduces overall network congestion and is simpler to manage, therefore reports should be more accurate. Reporting is just one step in a successful patch process. Accurately rating patch threat levels and proper patch application techniques are also required.

Management must resist the urge to unilaterally decree a security process without the participation of all interested parties. I can recall the resulting turmoil at one corporation I have worked with. Management asked the central security group to determine the patch application process. This group came up with a process, which required patches to be applied in a specific window of time (this window being determined by the level of threat that each patch was designed to address). Failure to apply a patch within a given window would result in a server being removed from the network. No system engineering or support groups were involved with defining the process or timeline. As you might imagine, the resulting issues caused more damage that any virus did.

The first time this process was implemented the security policies stated that all servers that were not patched were to be taken off the network.

Unfortunately, no patch was yet available. There was a workaround that would stop servers from getting infected, just no official Microsoft patch was yet available. Therefore, according to the policy, security started to take servers off the network, whether they were infected or not. This caused a major disruption in the company's ability to do business and hundreds of thousands of dollars were lost because uninfected servers were taken off the network.

Avoiding Common Mistakes

To avoid these types of mistakes, it is important that every party with a vested interest be included in the policy setting process. In some cases it may even be wise to include customers in creating the patch procedures. After all, if the network fails, it will undoubtedly affect them.

There is no single process that will work for every company. However, some simple guidelines can help ensure a policy that works well. Patches should be rated according to their threat level. Factors to consider include:

- Does the patch address a real or perceived security threat?
- Is the environment highly vulnerable? (i.e. a web farm would be more concerned with an IIS patch than a patch for MS SQL).
- Does the patch protect against an active exploit or virus that is currently in circulation?

When determining a timeline within which the patch should be applied, it is important not to fall into the trap of stipulating a predefined number of days to apply the patch. Take the example of an IT organization that establishes three classifications: Medium, High and Critical. Medium risk patches have to be installed within thirty days. High risk patches address verified threats for which an exploit existed, but are not active. These patches are to be applied within fifteen days. The Critical patch rating is for active attacks, like NIMDA and Code Red virus outbreaks.

This hypothetical IT department made these procedures without consulting the groups who actually managed and supported the servers. After all, thirty days is more than enough time to test and apply one patch. One patch, yes. Problems begin to arise when multiple server patches are released within a few days of each other. Each patch has to be applied within thirty days of its being rated. This results in support personnel having to manage a storm of patches, all in different stages of being applied. Add to that the fact that some patches supercede others or required service packs before they can be applied and one can begin to see the problems that can arise. To address this time constraint, support personnel have two choices: give up sleep and work continual long hours to get each patch tested and applied, or lie about their progress and wait for patches to supercede each other, so only the newest patches would be applied.

There are several ways to address this problem. Here are two solutions that work for web servers as well as any large enterprise. The first is to have the team that rates patches determine the patch application due date on a case-by-case basis. If several patches are released close together, this team would determine which to apply first and how quickly it must be applied. If a patch is not critical and is expected to be superceded by a new patch in a few weeks, they might decide to hold off on implementation altogether. With this type of solution, it is critical that every department is represented on the team; this is required to maintain a complete understanding of the environment.

Some organizations have had great success with setting up standard patch deployment windows. Under this type of patch deployment program, patches are queued and applied at regular intervals, say, quarterly. This process can work well, as the deployment windows can be timed not to conflict with critical company events, such as an annual website sales event, or financial close periods. This ensures that if an issue is encountered, it will not occur during a critical period of time. Furthermore, because patches queue, superceded patches can simply be skipped as long as the newest version is installed.

The downside to this method is that the network could be exposed to moderate security risks for a longer period of time. To mitigate this risk, any critical patches, like active threats, can be patched immediately, out of the normal cycle. Additionally, if a patch that is waiting for the next release period to be applied suddenly becomes a more prominent threat, it can always be re-evaluated and applied sooner, if needed.

This is the only method of patch deployment outlined here that helps project managers and system engineers plan their implementation around patch deployment windows. Because of this, it fits well in to the project life cycle used by most large corporations and helps insure application stability.

Automated Patching

The typical patch application process is very resource-intensive. An administrator logs into a server, downloads the patch, applies the patch, reboots the server, validates that the patch has been applied successfully, validates the server's application functions are as expected (i.e. that the website is still reachable), records this information, and then moves on to the next server. This is a very time-consuming process and is the reason why some IT departments opt to push patches out via SMS or a similar utility, even if this process is not reliable. They simply don't have enough personnel to manually patch, test, and validate each server.

By automating patch deployment we can reduce the amount of time it takes to apply patches. This can be done without spending expensive resources developing a custom patching application. Since we are talking about a decentralized deployment solution, simple scripting can accomplish this task. Each department within a large IT organization can manage a subset of servers; say for example, 100 servers per department. Often, it is logical to have each department simply patch the servers that they manage.

Example Code

Below is a sample script that can be used to patch many servers at one time. With a little modification, it can be used to apply multiple patches to entire groups of servers.

```
1  ::  Set the name of the server to be patched
2  set servername=Foo
3  ::  Set the name of the patch
4  set patch=samplepatch.exe
5  ::  Time, use 24 hour standard
6  set time=14:35
7  @echo on
8  copy %patch% \\%servername%\c$\temp /z
9  at \\%servername% %time% c:\temp\%patch% /s
```

This script is designed to be run from a workstation and uses the logged in user's right. Therefore , the account that is logged on to the machine that runs the script must have administrative rights on all the servers to be patched.

Line #2 sets the server name to the variable 'server'.

Line #4 sets the name of the patch to be applied. In this case samplepatch.exe

Line #6 sets the time for the patch to be applied using a 24-hour clock.

Line #8 copies the patch to the target's server's

c:\temp folder

Line #9 sets up an AT command to apply the patch at 2:35 PM the next day.

Once the script runs, the output should be checked for error messages. This script can be set up to patch a large group of servers using a simple FOR loop. The script can also be modified to automatically reboot servers using shutdown.exe, included with the Microsoft Resource Kit. It can even run qchain.exe to avoid any DLL conflicts when applying multiple patches on Windows NT and 2000. Windows 2003 has DLL conflict detection code built-in, so running qchain.exe is not necessary. For NT 4 and 2000 systems, qchain.exe can be downloaded from Microsoft.com

After this automated tool patches and reboots each server, verification is still needed. Verifying that the application is still functioning as expected is normally as simple as having someone try to load a webpage, or access a database. However, we still need to automate the tasks of verifying that the patch was applied successfully.

Several tools are available to automatically check patch deployment status. Many are unreliable. Patch verification tools should use several different methods to verify that a patch has been successfully applied. Some tools can provide customized reports detailing the patch state of groups of servers. Other tools provide exporting capabilities to make centralizing reports simple. Since licensing costs for these products can be prohibitive, obtain a shareware version for testing, if possible.

Alternative options include homegrown applications, or small scripts to verify successful patching. WMI or VB scripts are ideal for this type of testing. These scripts can be configured to check DLL versions, registry entries as well as patch log files to validate a patch was applied without problems.

Summary

Well thought-out security threat response plans will include all players in the planning and rating processes. Everyone's participation is required to ensure a complete picture of the environment. Most large enterprises will benefit from using a decentralized security patch deployment process. One of the most important factors to remember is to leverage automation as much as possible. Automation opportunities include virus software, patching and patch checking tools. Automate as much of the routine work as possible, to reduce the resources required to maintain server security.

Appendix

IIS 6.0 Basic Website Configuration

This appendix covers the basic website settings in IIS 6.0, most of which have not changed from IIS 5.0. Chapter 5, *Application and Website Configuration*, discusses many of the new options available in IIS 6.0. This appendix will be of interest to first time IIS users and readers who need a refresher.

The **Web Site** tab (figure A.1) configures The IP address information for the website. The **advanced** button allows for multiple websites to be configured on a single IP address, as discussed in detail in Chapter 5. The **TCP port** number is normally left to the default, port 80. If the website uses SSL, then the **SSL Port** should be set to 443.

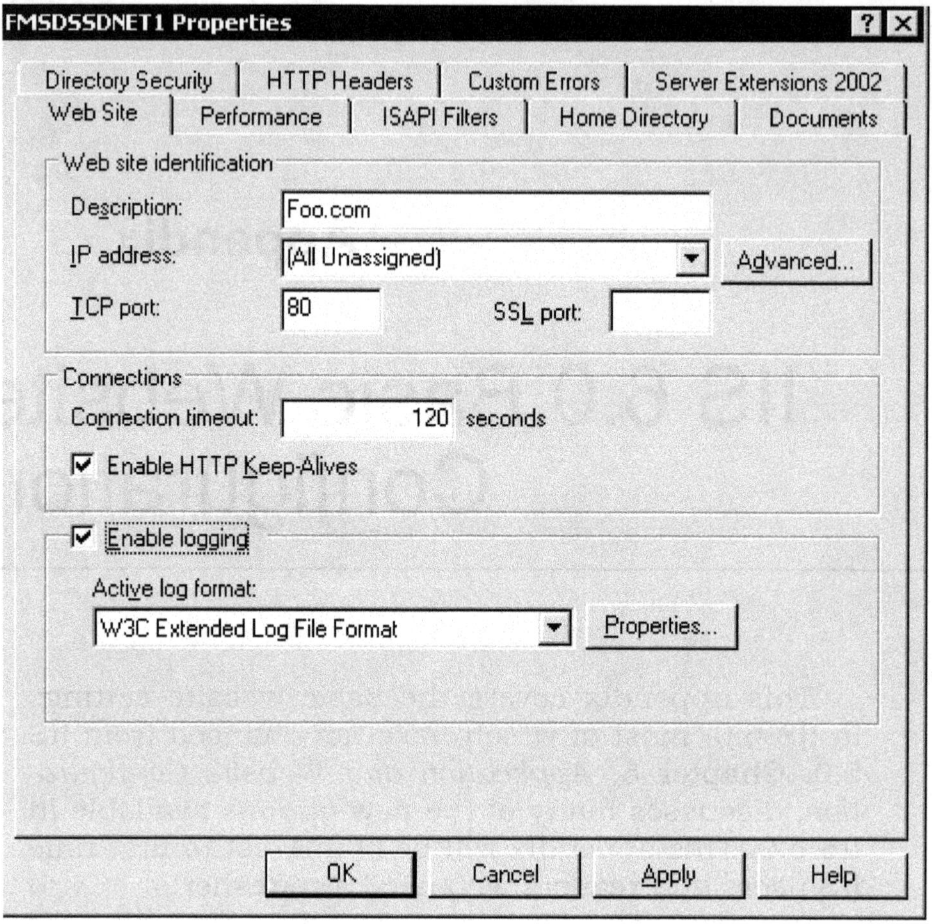

Figure A.1 Web Site

For **HTTP Keep-Alives** the default of 120 seconds, is usually sufficient. However, under some circumstances this time may need to be lengthened or shortened. For example, if users download large web pages that might take longer than two minutes to complete, then extending the **HTTP Keep-Alives** time may provide improved performance.

The **enable logging** option specifies whether the website will maintain an access log. The **properties** button allows an administrator to determine what information is logged and where the log files will be stored.

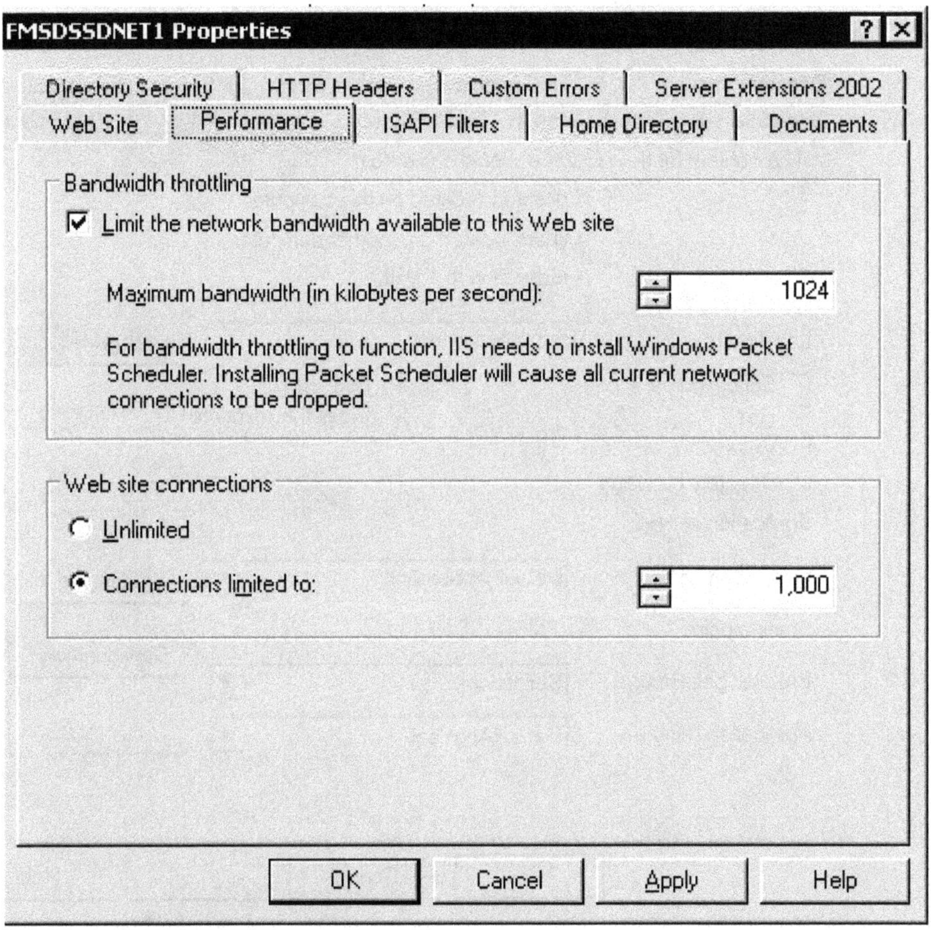

Figure A.2 Performance

The **Performance** tab (figure A.2) in IIS 6.0 allows the enabling of bandwidth throttling, as well as limiting the number of website connections. Both settings are useful for ensuring that one website does not monopolize the resources on the entire server.

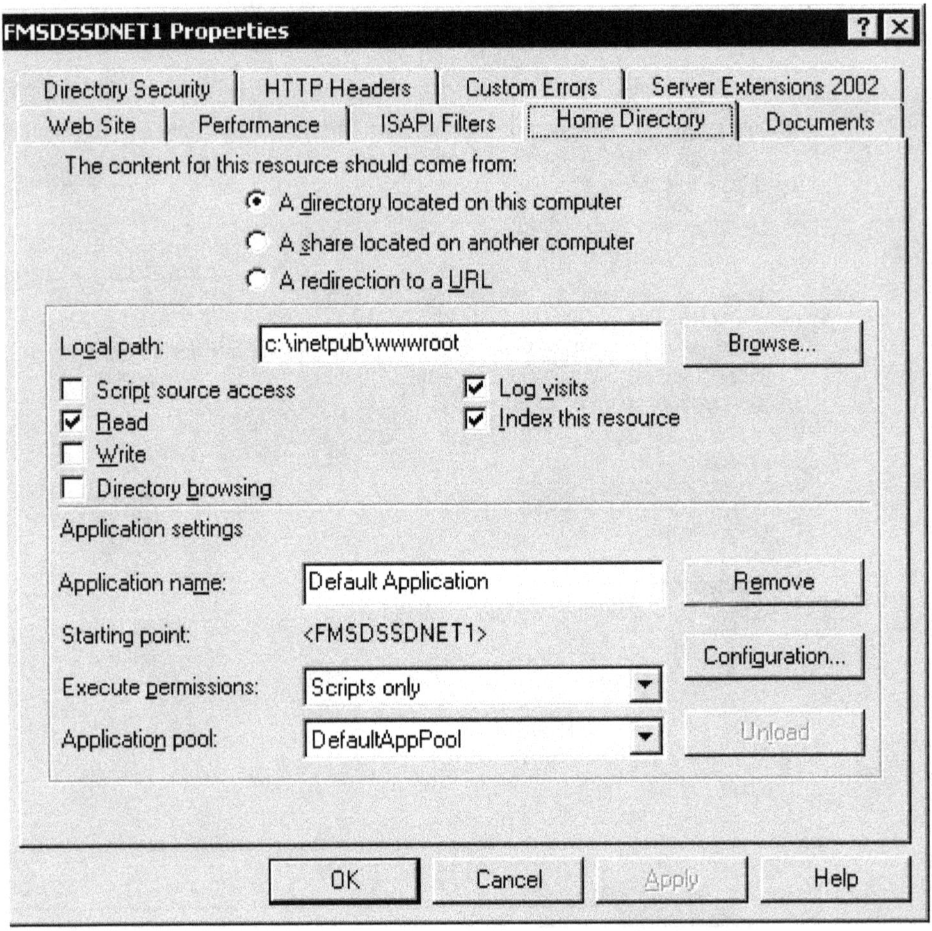

Figure A.3 Home Directory

The **Home Directory** tab, shown in figure A.3, allows the **Local Path** to be assigned. Access permissions can also be set from this tab. These settings include allowing or disabling:

- Directory browsing
- Script source access
- Write access
- Read access
- Log visits
- Index this resource

The **HTTP Headers** tab (figure A.4) allows an administrator to enable content expiration. Content expiration is convenient for time sensitive content, such as limited time offers. Once the content is expired a user's browser will purge the cached web page and reload it the next time the page is requested. Content can be set to expire immediately, after a specified number of days, or on a specific date.

Custom HTTP headers function differently than the document footer under the **Documents** tab. The HTTP headers option passes a value to the browser. The value is not displayed as part of the web page, as it is with the document footer. The Custom HTTP headers option allows commands to be sent to the browser that IIS 6.0 may not internally support.

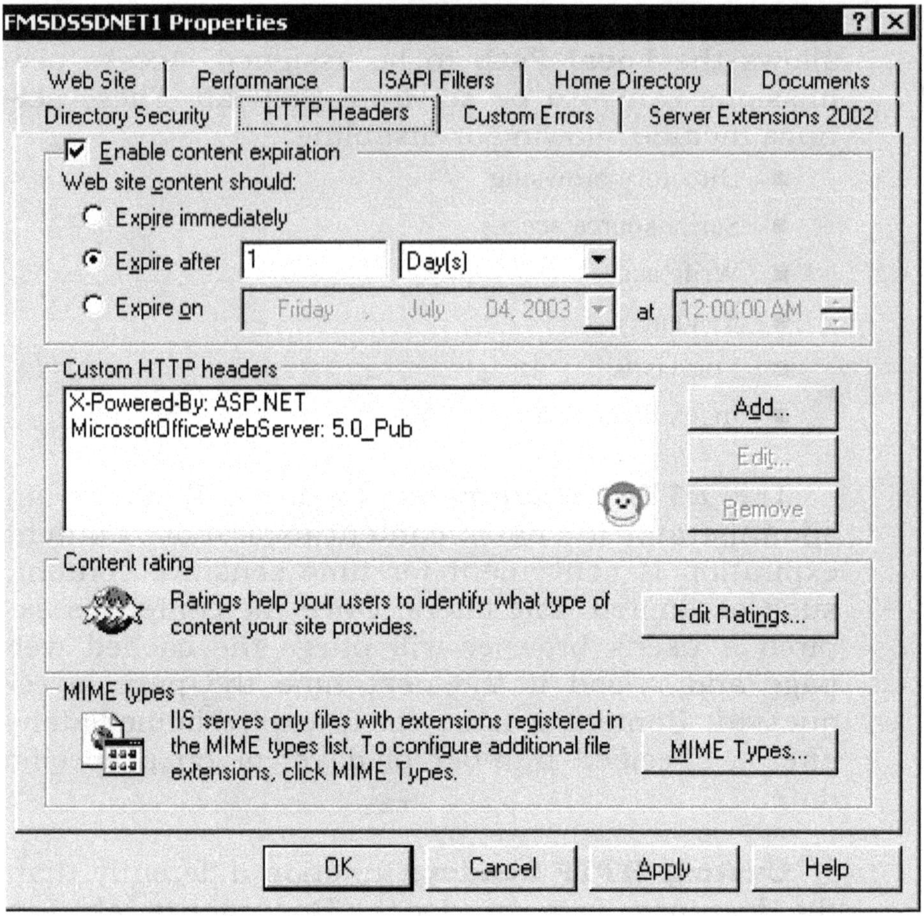

Figure A.4 HTTP Headers

Content rating allows a webmaster or adminis-trator to identify what type of content the website contains. Levels of violence, sex, nudity, and lan-guage can all be specified.

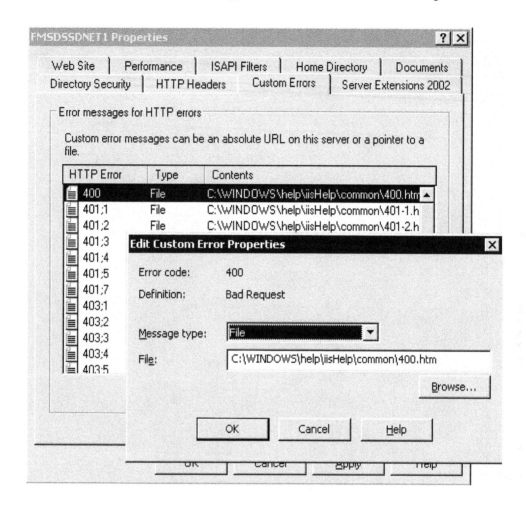

Figure A.5 Custom Errors

The **Custom Errors** tab, shown in figure A.5, can change the default error message to a custom message. The message can be a file or URL pointing to another web page. Custom error messages can be used to give users instructions on how to inform the administrator in the event of a failure, or error.

Notes